SKINNY DESSERTS

80 flavour-packed recipes
of less than 300 calories

Kathryn Bruton

Photography by Laura Edwards

Kyle Books

To our gorgeous girls Elsie and Lillie. Always know that you are wonderful,
that the sky is your limit, and you can achieve anything you put your mind to.

An Hachette UK Company
www.hachette.co.uk

First published in Great Britain in 2018 by Kyle
Books, an imprint of Kyle Cathie Ltd
Carmelite House
50 Victoria Embankment
London EC4Y 0DZ
www.kylebooks.co.uk

ISBN: 978 0 85783 480 5

Text copyright 2019 © Kathryn Bruton
Design and layout copyright 2019 © Kyle Cathie Ltd
Photography 2019 © Laura Edwards
Spine illustration 2019 © Kretsu Nataliya/Shutterstock
Endpaper illustration 2019 © Minur/Shutterstock

Distributed in the US by Hachette Book Group,
1290 Avenue of the Americas, 4th and 5th Floors,
New York, NY 10104

Distributed in Canada by Canadian Manda
Group, 664 Annette St., Toronto, Ontario,
Canada M6S 2C8

Kathryn Bruton is hereby identified as
the author of this work in accordance
with Section 77 of the Copyright,
Designs and Patents Act 1988.

Editor: Hannah Coughlin
Design: Louise Leffler
Photography: Laura Edwards
Food styling: Kathryn Bruton
Props styling: Tabitha Hawkins
Production: Nic Jones and Gemma John

A Cataloguing in Publication record for this
title is available from the British Library

Printed and bound in China

10 9 8 7 6 5 4 3 2 1

Nutritional information key:
DF – dairy-free
GF – gluten-free
V – vegetarian
VE – vegan

All nutritional information is given per serving.

contents

introduction

I believe with all of my heart that dessert should not feel like you are on a diet of any kind. A dessert should be indulgent, decadent, sweet and satisfying, in essence, a moment of extravagance, a moment to let loose and indulge without the burden of considering it's impact on your waistline. However, there must be a 'best of both worlds' compromise – recipes for desserts that are all we desire them to be, but without a humongous calorie count. Importantly, for me feel satisfied, this had to be possible without sacrificing any of the good stuff. I want each recipe to be enjoyed, safe in the knowledge that they are indeed low calorie, but on the surface not appearing to be. So while you are enjoying a white chocolate Creme brûlée or a rich and decadent chocolate mousse cake, you are not thinking that it is lacking something. Instead, you are simply enjoying how utterly delicious it is, wondering how on earth it could possibly be under 300 calories.

While writing this book, I short listed traditional recipes to redesign as well as hundreds of ideas for new ones. All that made the cut have had every ingredient endlessly considered. To bring the calorie counts down it was necessary to play around with quantities of high offenders such as butter, sugar, cream, chocolate – to substitute lower calorie ingredients or decrease the quantities. Take Passion Fruit Tarts for example (page 22). Slightly less butter is used in the pastry – not so much that to effect the recipe, but enough to impact the calorie count. The pastry is rolled thinly so is crisp when baked, and again, lower in calories than a thicker base. The filling is sharp and tart, using mainly fresh passion fruit juice, and the result is a tart which delivers absolutely everything you would want it to, but no more than 225 calories per portion. The Chocolate Mousse Cake (page 49) is one traditionally made with double cream, but I gave it a whirl with natural yogurt and it was simply perfect. Some might even prefer it's lighter, sharper flavour. I adore chocolate brownies – who doesn't? But they must be molten, sticky and almost impossibly chocolatey, and most likely calorie laden per mouthful. But, when teamed with a meringue base you get the best of both worlds with less than 300 calories!

When it comes to ingredients, I have not used either artificial sweeteners nor alternative sugars and flours. I don't cook with these on a day to day basis, so how to use them well is far from my area of expertise. And when it comes to desserts, I will often feel the desire to bake when I am using ingredients that are likely to be knocking around my kitchen already. My most desirable puddings are those made with classic ingredients such as butter, plain flour, sugar, butter, cream, eggs and chocolate, to name but a few, but with clever tweaking.

Day to day, calories are a small portion of what I feel makes a meal. Above all, it needs to be nutritionally balanced, and when the time calls for it, low calorie. When it comes to dessert, I am the kind of person who often throws caution to the wind and allows plenty of room for indulgence. It is not always a time to think about being nutritionally 'good', and these recipes offer the perfect middle ground – all the indulgence, none of the penance.

a few useful notes

Equipment

I have never had the most amazingly equipped kitchen for baking, and have generally fumbled by on very little. There are a few recipes in this book that require some select purchases, such as the rum babas (see page 83) and the angel food cake (see page 16). However, the basics that will see you through many recipes in this book are: a tried and tested free-standing electric mixer, a handheld whisk, bowls, spatulas and, a must-have, digital weighing scales. I don't estimate teaspoon and tablespoon measures, and will never fail to rely on my measuring spoons. Even when I think I know the correct quantity by eye, I am generally wrong, and such discrepancies can be the difference between a recipe succeeding and it failing. As far as cake tins and trays go, I have a few 20cm and 24cm (8in and 9 ½in) round spring-form tins, a couple of 20cm (8in) round cake tins and two Swiss roll tins. I have a selection of mini loose-based fluted tart tins, and a few larger ones. In short, don't be daunted if you feel ill-equipped to bake; the chances are that you are more prepared than you think you are.

Eggs

Medium and large eggs are used throughout the book. It is not necessarily one size fits all, so pay attention when reading recipes. There are some recipes that use raw eggs (such as the Caramelized Honey Semifreddo with Nectarines on page 116 and the Rich Chocolate Fennel Cream Pots with Pomegranate on page 52). Always use the freshest organic free-range eggs for such recipes, and be careful to not add these to an entertaining menu if you are catering for a lady who is pregnant.

When making meringues, I often find that I have a surplus of egg yolks, which I have great intentions of using, store in the fridge, and then inevitably forget about. Most big supermarkets now sell egg whites in cartons, which are enormously useful.

Vanilla

You can buy vanilla in many different forms: essence, paste, extract and, its most natural (and expensive) form, pods. Throughout this book, I use mostly pods. At times, you may see the use of vanilla bean paste, which in my mind is the next best thing to a pod, and more cost-effective. However, none of the aforementioned substitutes really match up to the depth of flavour you can achieve by scraping seeds directly from a moist, aromatic pod. When making desserts or baking, vanilla pods can be one of your greatest expenses, but are worth every penny, so splash out whenever you feel you can justify it — you won't regret it. To get a bit more bang for your buck, save the pods and store in a jar with some caster sugar. The flavour will infuse and you will have an intensely flavoured vanilla sugar to play around with. I also quite like adding them to bottles of spirits — whisky, brandy and rum all take well to a bit of vanilla.

When removing the seeds from a pod, use a small, sharp knife to cut down the length of the pod, cleanly cutting it in half. Then use the tip of the knife to carefully scrape out the seeds.

Chocolate

As a rule, I always opt for a 70 per cent cocoa solids content when I cook with dark chocolate. More importantly, I won't skimp on quality. There are lots of great chocolate brands that now produce really good-quality dark chocolate. Some are more expensive than others, but in general, you get what you pay for in terms of quality and flavour. Chocolate takes centre stage in its very own chapter here, and using top-notch stuff will really make a difference to the recipes.

Optional ingredients

There are certain recipes in this book that list decoration ingredients as optional. This is mostly where the addition of this extra ingredient will tip the calorie count over the 300 mark, but equally where the final dish will not actually suffer without it. In these instances, the decision is yours as to whether or not you go all out. I would advise it – it will never be much more than 300 calories, which is still a low calorie count for a pudding!

Greasing and lining tins and baking trays

Use some greaseproof paper to smear a very thin layer of butter all over the tin, including the sides, and then line the base of the tin with greaseproof paper. To be on the safe side, I always grease the paper, too.

Cream – single, double and whipping cream

Essentially these are all the same thing but have vastly different calorie counts. Single cream is, of course, the lowest at 188 calories per 100ml (3 ½fl oz). Double cream is the highest, boasting a whole 445 calories per 100ml (3 ½fl oz). And whipping cream, one that we often overlook, comes in at 370 calories per 100ml (3 ½fl oz). These calorie counts will differ slightly depending on the brand you're using, but in general will follow this pattern. There are certain instances where a specific type of cream must be used. Single cream cannot be whipped, which renders it useless for many dessert recipes, unless you need a pouring cream, for which it is perfect. In many places in the book, where a whipped cream is needed I have often chosen whipping cream rather than double to save on calories.

Fatless sponge

A fatless sponge is made, as the name suggests, without fat. Whisking eggs and sugar to triple their volume helps to stabilize the mixture and the end result is a very light, fluffy and aerated sponge. Substituting this kind of sponge for one made with butter goes a long, long way towards reducing calorie content. It is used a few times through this book and the main thing to remember, in order to achieve success when making it, is to be as gentle and patient as you can. The air created when whisking the eggs and sugar to triple their volume is integral to achieving a risen, aerated sponge, so you must try to knock out as little air as possible when folding in the flour. I use a big balloon whisk for this as it helps to cut through the flour and disperse it more evenly, meaning the overall process is quicker and more efficient.

Have fun

We have all had failed attempts when baking or making any kind of dessert. I include myself in this and there has been many a time when I have had to tackle a recipe a second or even a third time. The truth is, though this is a rare enough occurrence, it can knock your confidence and put you off trying again. Don't let that be the case. To give yourself every chance at succeeding the first time, read the recipe a few times and have all of your ingredients laid out before you start, and always ensure your oven is preheated when necessary. And, as with all cooking, enjoy it.

cakes, tarts and pies

Few things are more tempting than lusciously layered cakes, such as a rhubarb, cardamom and ginger one, drenched in cream and spilling over with fruit. When the main meal finds itself served up in the middle of the day, a cake can be the perfect way to wrap it up. A cup of tea to accompany is a must! If your penchant is for a sticky, gooey, oozy cake, the Verjuice, Pear, Vanilla and Thyme Upside Down Cake gives you a substantial chunk of utter indulgence. Then there are, of course, the citrus tart fans — no doubt you could be tempted by a vibrant passion fruit version. And if none of the above tickles your fancy, perhaps a mile-high meringue layered pie might tempt you? If not, surely a devilishly chocolatey bitter chocolate torte must get your taste buds dancing.

This chapter is packed with desserts that will leave you wondering where the calories are hiding. There are no secrets here — just thoughtful reimagining of classic recipes and clever new ones. A fatless sponge teamed with delicious rhubarb to make a tiered exposed cake, punctuated by set rhubarb syrup and filled with fresh rhubarb, cream and yogurt. A cheat's tart with an easy-to-make ginger biscuit base, filled with a sharp but warming ginger pannacotta filling; with no baking it's great for easy entertaining. Plump satsumas simmered in a luscious bay-infused syrup, topped with fluffy meringue which becomes light and crisp when baked; the result is sweet and sticky but light as a feather. Or one of my favourites — the baked Lemon Cheesecake with Roasted Plums. It comes out of the oven in a blaze of glory, and gets topped with sweet roasted plums; this is an absolute must for cheesecake lovers.

Many of the recipes in this chapter were created with sheer indulgence in mind as that's what we want from a cake, tart or pie, right? Have your cake, eat it, and do so in the reassuring knowledge that it is seriously low in calories.

bitter chocolate, pistachio and pomegranate torte

Considering this torte isn't overly sweet it is deliciously decadent. The combination of bitter dark chocolate with sweet and sour pomegranate molasses is somewhat addictive, the flavours harmonize beautifully. And ground pistachios create a beautiful texture. You don't need much of this to feel satisfied, and a spoonful of natural yogurt finishes it off perfectly.

Serves 12

 calories 284 GF V

Carbs 19g   Sugar 18.5g   Protein 5g   Fibre 0.5g   Fat 20.5g   Sat Fat 10g   Salt trace

200g (7oz) dark chocolate, minimum 70% cocoa solids
150g (5½ oz) unsalted butter
2 tablespoons pomegranate molasses
100g (3½oz) shelled pistachios
4 medium eggs
80g (3oz) caster sugar

To serve
natural yogurt
pomegranate seeds

Preheat the oven to 180°C/350°F/gas mark 4. Grease and line a 24cm (9½in) round spring-form tin with greaseproof paper. Break the chocolate into small pieces and place in a heatproof bowl with the butter and pomegranate molasses. Place over a pan of simmering water, ensuring the base is not touching the water. Stir occasionally and when melted, set aside to cool.

Place the pistachios into a small handheld food-processor and blitz until you have a fine powder. Separate the eggs into two medium bowls. Place half of the sugar into the bowl with the yolks, and using a handheld electric whisk, beat until thick and creamy. Wash and dry the whisks and then whisk the egg whites. When they are starting to thicken, add the remaining sugar, and then continue whisking until the mixture is stiff, thick and glossy.

Using a large metal spoon, gently fold the melted chocolate into the egg yolk mixture, followed by the ground pistachios. Carefully and patiently fold in the egg whites, one third at a time. Transfer to the prepared tin, scraping out all the mixture with a rubber spatula.

Bake for 20–25 minutes. Allow to cool slightly in the tin before removing. This is best served warm with a spoonful of natural yogurt and some fresh pomegranate seeds.

peach and raspberry turnover tarts

These little handheld tarts are filled with a deliciously sweet
fruit compote. Great as a picnic dessert, they could also be served
with melted chocolate for dipping.

Makes 10

Carbs 23g   Sugar 7.5g   Protein 4.5g   Fibre 2g   Fat 10.5g   Sat Fat 5g   Salt trace

200g (7oz) plain flour,
plus extra for dusting
90g (3¼oz) chilled unsalted
butter, cut into cubes
a few drops of almond extract
(optional)
1 medium egg, beaten
1 tablespoon caster sugar

For the filling
3 fresh peaches, halved, stoned
and roughly chopped
70g (2½oz) raspberries
45g (1½oz) maple syrup
1 vanilla pod, halved and seeds
scraped out
40g (1½oz) flaked almonds

Pulse the flour and butter in a food-processor until
it resembles breadcrumbs. Add 3 tablespoons of water
and the almond extract, if using, and pulse again until
it comes together. Don't overwork it, or it will be tough.
Knead briefly on a smooth surface and flatten into a
disc. Wrap in clingfilm and refrigerate for 30 minutes.

Place the peaches, raspberries, maple syrup and vanilla
pod with seeds in a small saucepan over a medium heat.
Simmer slowly until the fruit starts to break down,
about 5 minutes. Increase the heat and boil for about
7 minutes, until the liquid is thick and syrupy. Remove
from the heat and cool. Toast the almonds in a dry
frying pan until golden, then stir through and set aside.

Remove the pastry from the fridge and allow to soften
slightly at room temperature for a few minutes. Dust a
clean surface with a little flour and roll out until 5mm
(¼in) thick all over. Cut out as many discs as you can,
about 10–13cm (4–5in) wide, transfer to a baking
tray lined with greaseproof paper, then refrigerate to
stop the pastry from softening too much. Gather the
remaining dough, and repeat. You should be able to
get ten discs in total.

Place 1 tablespoon of filling onto the centre of each
disc. Brush a little water across the edge of each and fold
over, pressing hard to seal. Brush with a little beaten
egg, sprinkle with caster sugar and pierce a small hole in
the top of each. Bake for 20 minutes, or until golden.

coffee chocolate angel food cakes

Angel food cake is nothing more than whisked egg whites with flour and sugar folded in. It couldn't be easier to make and is as light as a feather. These boast some pretty indulgent decorations, too.

Makes 6

calories 236

V

Carbs 43g   Sugar 33g   Protein 5g   Fibre 1g   Fat 5g   Sat Fat 2.5g   Salt 0.2g

10g (½oz) butter, for greasing
75g (2½oz) plain flour, plus
   extra for dusting
6 egg whites
½ teaspoon cream of tartar
135g (4¾oz) caster sugar
I teaspoon chicory and coffee
   essence (such as Camp)
60g (1¾oz) dark chocolate,
   minimum 70% cocoa solids,
   broken into pieces
40g (1½oz) honeycomb, finely
   chopped or blitzed (see page
   139)
chocolate-covered coffee
   beans, roughly chopped,
   to serve (optional)

Preheat the oven to 180°C/350°F/gas mark 4 and place a 6-hole mini bundt tin in the fridge. Melt the butter, then, with a pastry brush, thinly coat the inside of each mould with a little butter. Return to the fridge for a few minutes and then repeat. This step is helpful because when the tin is cold, the butter hardens as you brush it on, making it easier to ensure you have greased all of the little corners. Dust with a little flour and set aside.

Place the egg whites and cream of tartar in an electric stand mixer and whisk until soft peaks form. Add 80g (3oz) of the sugar, I tablespoon at a time, and continue whisking for a few minutes. Whisk in the coffee essence.

Add the remaining sugar to the flour and sift it twice. When the egg whites are ready, sift the flour and sugar one last time all over the mixture, and then very gently fold it in. Transfer to a piping bag and pipe into the moulds, ensuring that they are thoroughly filled (the mixture shrinks when cooked, so filling the tin is important). Alternatively, spoon the mixture in. Bake for 10–15 minutes, or until light golden brown.

When ready, turn the tin upside down onto a wire rack. The cakes should come away easily, but a little tap will encourage them. Allow to cool completely.

Melt the chocolate in a bowl over a pan of gently simmering water. Place a baking tray lined with greaseproof paper underneath the cakes, then drizzle over the chocolate. Dust with the honeycomb and top with chocolate-covered coffee beans, if desired.

lemon cheesecake with roasted plums

This cheesecake is a touch of delicate decadence.
It is the essence of simplicity, in all of its glory.

Serves 10

calories
251

V

Carbs 25g   Sugar 21.5g   Protein 12g   Fibre 1g   Fat 11g   Sat Fat 5.5g   Salt 0.4g

650g (13oz) soft Italian ricotta
150g (5oz) golden caster sugar,
   plus 10g (½oz) for dusting
50g (1¾oz) plain flour
zest of 4 lemons
juice of 1 lemon
6 large eggs, separated
pinch of salt
5 plums, stoned and cut into
   wedges
juice of 1 orange
1 tablespoon clear honey
crème fraîche, to serve
   (optional)

Preheat the oven to 180°C/350°F/gas mark 4. Grease and line a 20cm (8in) round spring-form tin. In an electric stand mixer, gently whip the ricotta until smooth. Add half of the sugar, the flour, lemon zest and juice, egg yolks and salt. Beat again until smooth.

In a separate bowl, whisk the egg whites until soft peaks form, and then gradually add the remaining sugar, continually whisking until thick and glossy. Gently fold half of the egg white mixture into the ricotta until just combined. Fold in the rest and then pour into the prepared tin. Bake for 50 minutes, covering with foil if it begins to brown too much. Allow to cool completely in the tin before removing.

Toss the plums with the orange juice and honey in a roasting tray, then roast for about 10–15 minutes until tender, but still holding their shape.

Slice the cake and serve each slice with plums alongside and a spoon of crème fraîche, if using.

orange yogurt cakes with pomegranate glaze

These little cakes are such a treat. The zest of two oranges looks like a lot, but without it, the cakes miss that definitive orange flavour that makes them special.

Serves 4

Carbs 37g   Sugar 22g   Protein 6g   Fibre 1g   Fat 8g   Sat Fat 1.5g   Salt 0.4g

60g (2oz) caster sugar
zest of 2 oranges, plus extra
   to decorate
1 tablespoon orange juice
sprig of rosemary, leaves picked
75g (2½oz) plain flour
pinch of bicarbonate of soda
¼ teaspoon baking powder
140g (5oz) natural yogurt
30ml (1fl oz) vegetable oil
1 medium egg
150ml (5fl oz) pomegranate
   juice
pomegranate seeds, to decorate
   (optional)

Preheat the oven to 180°C/350°F/gas mark 4. Line four 9.5 x 6.8 x 4.2cm (3¾ x 2½ x 1⅔in) mini cake or loaf tins with greaseproof paper.

Place the caster sugar, orange zest, juice and rosemary in a saucepan over a medium heat. Stir from time to time, and when the sugar is dissolved and you have a nice clear syrup, set aside and leave to cool completely.

Sift the flour, bicarbonate of soda and baking powder into a bowl. In a separate bowl, mix together half the yogurt with the vegetable oil and egg. Pass the syrup through a sieve and stir into this mixture. Add the dry ingredients to the wet ingredients and mix together until there are no lumps in the mixture.

Divide the mixture between the prepared mini cake tins and bake for 15 minutes on the middle shelf of the oven. When ready, allow to cool slightly in the tins and then transfer to a wire rack.

Simmer the pomegranate juice in a small saucepan until reduced to about 50ml (1¾fl oz). It will be thick and syrupy. Allow to cool completely.

To serve, top each cake with a spoonful of the remaining yogurt and drizzle the pomegranate syrup on top. Decorate with some fresh pomegranate seeds and a little orange zest.

passion fruit tarts

This recipe was inspired by a passion fruit tart I ate at a French patisserie in London. I wanted to recreate the intense flavour of passion fruit presented in a tart, but without the butter-laden filling. If you are a fan of desserts that are not overly sweet, this is the one for you.

Makes 6

 calories 225 V

Carbs 28g   Sugar 16g   Protein 8g   Fibre 1g   Fat 9g   Sat Fat 4.5g   Salt 0.3g

For the pastry

50g (1¾oz) butter, plus extra for greasing

125g (4½oz) flour, plus extra for dusting

25g (1oz) icing sugar

1 medium egg yolk

¾ tablespoon ice-cold water

For the filling

15 passion fruit (yielding about 160ml/5½fl oz juice)

100g (3½oz) 0% fat Greek yogurt

70g (2½oz) clear honey

3 eggs

70g (2½oz) raspberries, to decorate

icing sugar, to dust (optional)

Rub the butter into the flour and icing sugar until it resembles breadcrumbs. Add the egg yolk and use a knife to cut it through the flour. Add the water and continue until it starts to come together. Tip out onto a clean work surface and bring together with your hands to form a relatively smooth dough. Roll into a sausage shape and cut into six equal pieces. Place one between pieces of greaseproof paper, flatten out and repeat with the other pieces. Refrigerate for at least 1 hour.

Grease six 10cm (4in) round fluted tart tins with a little butter and dust with flour. Roll out one disc of pastry to 5mm (¼in) thick. Gently press into a tin and trim the edges with a sharp knife. Repeat with the remaining dough, then chill for 30 minutes–1 hour in the fridge. You can complete this step the day or night before.

Preheat the oven to 180°C/350°F/gas mark 4. Place a piece of greaseproof paper in each case and fill with baking beans, or similar. Bake for 15 minutes, remove the baking beans, then bake for another 10 minutes.

For the filling, scoop out the passion fruits into a small blender. Blitz to break up the seeds then pass through a sieve, pressing with the back of a spoon to extract as much juice as possible. Add the yogurt and honey and mix well. Whisk in the eggs immediately before using.

Pour into the tart cases and bake for a further 15–20 minutes, until set with a slight wobble. Allow to cool, then top with raspberries and icing sugar and serve.

plum galette with orange and ricotta

This free-form tart celebrates the beautiful plum. They need little more than a touch of orange zest and honey to bring out their best. Don't be too precious when it comes to shaping; confidently fold over the fruit, crimping together tightly where the pastry overlaps. The aim here is rustic charm!

Serves 10

 calories 244

Carbs 35g   Sugar 17g   Protein 3.5g   Fibre 2g   Fat 10g   Sat Fat 6g   Salt trace

For the pastry
230g (8oz) plain flour, plus extra for dusting
50g (1¾oz) caster sugar
100g (3½oz) chilled unsalted butter
zest of 1 orange, plus extra to decorate
1 teaspoon apple cider vinegar
65ml (2½fl oz) ice-cold water

For the filling
100g (3½oz) soft Italian ricotta
zest of ½ orange
50g (1¾oz) caster sugar
8 medium plums, halved, stoned and thinly sliced
1 tablespoon milk, for brushing
2 tablespoons clear honey

Blitz the flour, sugar, butter and orange zest in a food-processor until it resembles fine breadcrumbs. Add the vinegar and water and blitz until the dough just comes together. Flatten out between two pieces of greaseproof paper and refrigerate for at least 30 minutes.

Preheat the oven to 200°C/400°F/gas mark 6 and place a baking tray inside to get hot. This will help the galette cook evenly from top and bottom – without this the base of the tart may not cook properly, particularly in the middle.

Mix the ricotta with the orange zest and 20g (¾oz) of the sugar. Remove the pastry from the fridge and dust a clean flat surface with flour. Roll the pastry out into a long oval shape until it is about 5mm (¼in) thick all over. Transfer to a piece of greaseproof paper about the same size as the tray you are going to cook the tart on. Spread the ricotta mixture all over, leaving a 2.5cm (1in) border. Lay the plum slices on top and fold over the edges. Brush with a little milk, sprinkle all over with the remaining sugar, including the pastry edges, and bake for 30 minutes. Drizzle the honey all over the fruit and bake for a further 10 minutes. Sprinkle with extra orange zest and serve warm.

cardamom, honey and rose milk tart

This is very similar to a custard tart; delicate, light, aromatic and easy to make. A drizzle of honey fresh from the comb and a dusting of cinnamon are great additions, or it's lovely as is. To go all out, finish with bee pollen.

Serves 8

 calories 258 V

Carbs 29g   Sugar 11.5g   Protein 7g   Fibre 1g   Fat 12g   Sat Fat 7g   Salt 0.35g

For the pastry

100g (3½oz) chilled unsalted
  butter, cut into cubes
250g (9oz) plain flour, sifted
50g (2oz) icing sugar, sifted
1 medium egg yolk, gently
  whisked
2–3 tablespoons ice-cold water

For the filling

butter, for greasing
15g (½oz) plain flour, plus
  extra for dusting
15 cardamom pods, roughly
  pounded in a pestle and
  mortar
450ml (16fl oz) semi-skimmed
  milk
30g (1oz) clear honey
pared rind of 1 lemon
1 vanilla pod, halved and seeds
  scraped out
¼ teaspoon rosewater
2 large eggs
15g (½oz) cornflour

Rub the butter into the flour and icing sugar until the mixture resembles fine breadcrumbs. Add the egg yolk and water, 1 tablespoon at a time. Using a knife, cut through the mixture until it starts to come together (alternatively, use a food-processor). Add 1 more tablespoon of water if necessary. Tip the dough out and bring together with your hands, working quickly and gently. Shape into a rectangle, wrap in greaseproof paper and refrigerate for 30 minutes.

Preheat the oven to 180°C/350°F/gas mark 4. Grease a 35 x 12cm (14 x 5in) loose-based rectangular tart tin with butter and dust with flour. Roll out the pastry until it is 5mm (¼in) thick, then line the tin with it and trim away any excess. Chill for 30 minutes. Gently prick the pastry case with a fork, then place a piece of greaseproof paper in the case and fill with baking beans, or similar. Bake for 20 minutes, remove the baking beans and greaseproof paper and bake for another 10 minutes, until pale golden. Allow to cool.

Place the cardamom, milk, honey, lemon rind and vanilla pod and seeds in a saucepan and simmer for 15 minutes. Add rosewater to taste; remember it is very strong and can be overpowering. Sieve the mixture and clean the saucepan to remove any traces of cardamom.

In a large bowl, whisk the eggs, cornflour and flour until smooth. Pour in the warm milk while whisking. Return to the saucepan and heat gently until thick enough to coat a spoon. Pour into the cool case and bake for 15–20 minutes, until set with a slight wobble.

tangy ginger panna cotta tart with a chocolate crust

You might argue this is a bit of a cheat — an impressive tart put together without any fuss. The panna cotta-style filling is so delicate it is cloud-like, but the flavour is powerful, the spice and warmth of ginger lingering on your palate. It takes a little while to set so I would recommend making this the night before you plan to serve it, or the morning of.

Serves 10

calories
171

Carbs 27g   Sugar 18g   Protein 6g   Fibre 0.5g   Fat 4g   Sat Fat 1.5g   Salt 0.25g

For the crust
200g (7oz) ginger nut biscuits
20g (¾oz) cocoa powder

For the filling
100g (3½oz) caster sugar
50g (1¾oz) fresh ginger,
   peeled and finely chopped
300ml (10fl oz) almond milk
3 gelatine leaves
400g (14oz) 0% fat Greek
   yogurt

Grease and line a 20cm (8in) loose-based cake tin. For the crust, blitz the biscuits and cocoa in a food-processor until fine. Add 2½ tablespoons of water and pulse until combined. Tip the mixture into the prepared cake tin, and using the back of a spoon or your fingers, press evenly over the base and up the sides. Refrigerate while you prepare the filling.

Place the sugar and 100ml (3½fl oz) water in a small saucepan and heat until the sugar has dissolved. Add the ginger and simmer for about 10 minutes, until the liquid has reduced and is thick and syrupy. Add the almond milk and simmer for another 5 minutes. Set aside to cool a little. Soak the gelatine leaves in cold water for 5 minutes.

Strain the hot almond milk into a bowl. Remove the gelatine from the water and squeeze out any excess water. Whisk into the hot almond milk and then add this to the Greek yogurt, mixing until everything is combined. Pour into the cake tin, and refrigerate until set. This will take about 6 hours.

tartes fine aux pommes

This classic French pastry really captures the essence of apples
and is the perfect autumnal dessert. You can leave out the Calvados
if you don't have it to hand, or substitute with brandy.

Makes 4

calories
293

Carbs 34g   Sugar 21.5g   Protein 3g   Fibre 2g   Fat 13g   Sat Fat 7g   Salt 0.4g

3 Granny Smith apples
1 tablespoon Calvados
160g (5½oz) ready-rolled
   all-butter puff pastry
   (½ 320g/11oz packet)
flour, for dusting
juice of 1 lemon
15g (½oz) unsalted butter
15g (½oz) golden syrup
1 tablespoon vanilla bean paste
milk, for brushing
20g (¾oz) caster sugar

Cut a sheet of greaseproof paper to fit a large baking
tray, then place just the tray into the oven. This ensures
the bottom of the tarts begin to bake immediately.

Peel and core one of the apples; slice thinly. Place in
a small saucepan with 1 tablespoon of water, cover,
then place over a medium heat and simmer for about
7 minutes until soft. Add the Calvados and blitz until
smooth. Refrigerate in a bowl to chill completely.

Place the pastry on a lightly floured surface. Roll out big
enough to cut four circles using a 12cm (4½in) round
cookie cutter. Cut out four circles and transfer to the
greaseproof paper. Using a knife, draw a circle 1cm
(½in) inside the edge of the pastry. Chill until needed.

Squeeze the lemon juice into a bowl, removing any
seeds. Using a mandoline or very sharp knife, slice the
remaining cored apples very thinly into circles about
3mm (⅛in) thick. Toss in the lemon juice as you go.

When you are ready to make the tarts, preheat the oven
to 180°C/350°F/gas mark 4. Melt the butter, golden
syrup and vanilla bean paste together. Remove the pastry
and apple purée from the fridge. Divide the purée
between the tarts, and spread over the circle you have
drawn into the pastry. Arrange the apple slices on top
and brush the butter mixture all over. Clean the pastry
brush and dip into some milk to brush the edges of the
pastry, then sprinkle the edges with sugar.

Remove the hot baking tray from the oven and carefully
slide the greaseproof paper with the tarts onto it. Bake
for 15–20 minutes, or until golden brown.

caramel satsuma and bay meringue pie

A celebration of satsumas, this is a simple — yet far from standard — dessert. You could spice things up by adding a star anise and a cinnamon stick to the sugar syrup and switch the Cointreau for brandy or whisky.

Serves 6

calories 220   DF   GF   V

Carbs 50g   Sugar 50g   Protein 2.5g   Fibre 1g   Fat 0g   Sat Fat 0g   Salt 0.1g

12 satsumas
100g (3½oz) sugar
5 fresh bay leaves
1 tablespoon Cointreau
   (optional)
3 egg whites
pinch of salt
150g (5oz) caster sugar
¼ teaspoon cream of tartar

Peel each satsuma, removing as much of the stringy pith from the fruit as possible. Reserve 20g (¾oz) of peel and slice into very thin strips. Place this and the satsumas in a saucepan with the sugar, bay leaves and 100ml (3½fl oz) of water. Bring to the boil and simmer for 10 minutes, frequently turning over the satsumas. After the 10 minutes, carefully transfer the satsumas to a pie dish. Increase the heat slightly and boil the liquid until it is thick and syrupy and reduced by about half. Stir in the Cointreau, if using, and pour over the satsumas. Set aside while you prepare the meringue.

Place the egg whites in a clean bowl with a pinch of salt and whisk until soft peaks form. Add the sugar, 1 tablespoon at time, and then whisk until smooth, about 6–8 minutes. Add the cream of tartar and whisk briefly to combine.

Spread the meringue over the satsumas and bake for 20 minutes, or until the meringue is firm and slightly browned.

verjuice, pear, vanilla and thyme upside down cake

This is one of those cakes you will not want to share, and if it was 3000 calories per slice, it would be worth every bit of it. Verjuice may be hard to get your hands on in supermarkets but won't be a problem online. It is the juice of unripe grapes and is both sweet and gently acidic.

Serves 10

 calories 275

Carbs 36g   Sugar 27g   Protein 4g   Fibre 0.5g   Fat 13g   Sat Fat 6g   Salt 0.5g

250ml (9fl oz) verjuice
100g (3½oz) clear honey
1 vanilla pod, halved and seeds scraped out
8 sprigs of thyme
2 pared strips of lemon rind
3 pears
125ml (4fl oz) almond milk
110g (4oz) butter
115g (4oz) plain flour
50g (1¾oz) ground almonds
1 teaspoon bicarbonate of soda
140g (4¾oz) caster sugar
1 medium egg
80g (3oz) 0% fat Greek yogurt

Preheat the oven to 160°C/325°F/gas mark 3. Line a 20cm (8in) square, 7½cm (3in) deep tin with greaseproof paper, ensuring there are no holes.

Put the verjuice, honey, vanilla pod and seeds, thyme and lemon rind into a small saucepan over a high heat and simmer until reduced by half. Set aside to cool, while you prepare the remaining ingredients.

Quarter each pear, remove the cores, and slice thinly lengthways. Fan out and arrange on the base of the tin, ensuring there are minimal gaps. Pour over the syrup.

Place the almond milk and butter in a saucepan over a medium heat. When melted, allow to cool a little. Meanwhile, mix the flour, ground almonds, bicarbonate of soda and sugar in a bowl. In another bowl, whisk together the egg and yogurt. Mix the wet and dry ingredients together until thoroughly incorporated and then pour over the pears.

Place the cake tin on a baking tray and bake on the middle shelf of the oven for 35–40 minutes, or until a skewer comes out clean and the cake is golden brown.

Cool for about 5 minutes in the tin and then invert and remove to serve. The cake is so moist, it doesn't need to be served with anything, but a dollop of cream or crème fraîche never goes astray.

toffee apple sponge with calvados

This is a take on a dessert my mum used to make when I was young —
stewed apple topped with a fatless sponge and baked. For this recipe,
I have fried wedges of apple in butter, light brown sugar and Calvados,
creating a toffee-like coating and sauce that sits beneath a light and
fluffy sponge. Serve with custard or cream, or both if you are feeling
particularly indulgent.

Serves 8

 calories 291 V

Carbs 46g   Sugar 35g   Protein 6g   Fibre 1.5g   Fat 7.5g   Sat Fat 3.5g   Salt 0.4g

6 medium eating apples
juice of 1 lemon
40g (1½oz) unsalted butter
100g (3½oz) soft light brown
  sugar
50ml (2fl oz) Calvados
110g (4oz) caster sugar
4 medium eggs
seeds of 1 vanilla pod
115g (4oz) self-raising flour
1 teaspoon baking powder

Preheat the oven to 180°C/350°F/gas mark 4. Peel and
core the apples and cut each into eight wedges. Dress
with the lemon juice to stop them from browning. Melt
the butter in a heavy-based saucepan and add the apples
and brown sugar. Cook for 10 minutes, until the sugar
has dissolved and starts to coat the apples. Add the
Calvados and simmer for 5–7 minutes, until the sauce
is thick and syrupy. Transfer to a 22cm (9in) square,
4cm (1½in) deep baking dish.

Place the caster sugar, eggs and vanilla seeds in the
bowl of an electric stand mixer and whisk for about
7 minutes, until tripled in size. Sift the flour and
baking powder together and then sift again onto the
egg mixture. Very gently fold in using a balloon whisk,
lifting and dropping the mixture until everything is
evenly incorporated. You can also do this with a rubber
spatula. The most important thing is that you are
gentle and patient.

When ready, pour onto the apples. Bake for 25–30
minutes, or until a skewer inserted into the sponge
comes out clean. Serve warm.

rhubarb and cardamom layered cake

The decadant jelly in this gorgeous cake really captures the intense flavour of rhubarb, and makes a simple fatless sponge something truly special.

Serves 8

calories
276

Carbs 40g   Sugar 29g   Protein 7g   Fibre 2g   Fat 9.5g   Sat Fat 4.8g   Salt 0.4g

110g (4oz) caster sugar

4 medium eggs

115g (4oz) self-raising flour

1 teaspoon baking powder

1 teaspoon ground ginger

4 cardamom pods, seeds
  removed and finely ground

½ tablespoon icing sugar,
  for dusting

fresh edible flowers, to
  decorate (optional)

For the jelly

500g (18oz) forced rhubarb,
  cut into 5cm (2in) pieces

1 vanilla pod, halved lengthways

100g (3½oz) caster sugar

3 gelatine leaves, soaked in cold
  water for 5 minutes, then
  squeezed to remove excess
  water

For the cream filling

100ml (3½fl oz) whipping
  cream

100g (3½oz) Greek yogurt

Note: if you're short on time
or want a more simple cake,
omit the jelly and use the
rhubarb juice for a refreshing
drink such as bellinis, cocktails,
or mixed with sparkling water.

Preheat the oven to 180°C/350°F/gas mark 4. Line two 18cm (7in) round cake tins with clingfilm.

First make the jelly. Place the rhubarb, vanilla pod, sugar and 100ml (3½fl oz) water in a roasting dish. Roast for 15–20 minutes until soft, then separate the juice and set aside the fruit to cool. Whisk the squeezed gelatine into the hot juice then pour half into each prepared tin. Refrigerate to set.

Grease and line two more cake tins the same size. Whisk the sugar and eggs in an electric stand mixer on high for 7 minutes, until tripled in size, pale, thick and glossy. Sift the flour, baking powder, ginger and cardamom together, then sift over the whisked eggs. Use a balloon whisk to scoop up the mixture, then allow it to fall back. Very gently repeat this process until the flour is incorporated. Patience is key.

Divide the mixture between the prepared tins. Bake in the centre of the oven for 15 minutes, or until springy to the touch and a skewer inserted comes out clean. Cool in the tins for 5 minutes, then turn out onto to a wire rack.

Whip the cream until soft peaks form. Very gently fold in the Greek yogurt then chill until needed. Check that the jelly is set. Slice each cake in half horizontally. Place a circle of jelly on one half with the clingfilm facing up, then gently peel off. Top with another sponge. Spread almost half of the cream onto this sponge, and top with the chunks of rhubarb. Repeat with the remaining two sponges and layer of jelly. Scrape the remaining cream all around the sides of the cake. Dust with a little icing sugar and decorate with fresh edible flowers if you wish.

chocolate

I adore chocolate so much that it didn't feel enough to include it just here and there – it had to have its very own chapter. I was determined to make these recipes as indulgent as I possibly could. Chocolate wouldn't seem right dressed up as anything else.

There are lighter offerings, in the form of the White Chocolate, Blueberry and Lemon Jellies and the White Chocolate, Melon and Mint Fruit Salad. The latter is a particularly good choice in warmer months. Imagine this in a big bowl being served on the garden table after a huge barbecue. There are also a couple of classics in the form of White Chocolate Crème Brûlée and White Chocolate Rice Pudding with Vanilla Honey Figs. In their traditional form, crème brûlée and rice pudding are far from being low in calories, but making a few little tweaks here and there has achieved this. The good news is that you won't actually notice!

I have to admit, however, that this chapter is mostly designed with my own greedy appetite in mind. No matter how full I am, I will always opt for the most intensely chocolatey overindulgent dessert on the menu. And so, recipes such as the Chocolate Meringue Brownie, Rich Chocolate Fennel Cream Pots with Pomegranate, Chocolate Mousse Cake and Popcorn and Caramel Eclairs were created.

The chocolate meringue brownie has become a staple in my house. A casing of meringue filled with oozing chocolate brownie mixture, baked until it is just set. It is the absolute best of a brownie and of a meringue all blended into one. Chocolate fennel cream pots are one of those desserts you can whip up in a matter of minutes, prepare ahead and then lose yourself in. And if you are the chocoholic I am, you absolutely must make the chocolate mousse cake. It is deliciously light in texture, but the chocolate hit is like nothing else. It appears as shameless as you want a chocolate dessert to be.

cherry chocolate madeleines

These are a very simple sweet treat made even better by the addition of some melted chocolate for dipping. The method of greasing the tin below works really well and is worth doing for perfectly-shaped madeleines.

Makes 12/Serves 6

 calories 245

 V

Carbs 29g   Sugar 21g   Protein 4.5g   Fibre 1g   Fat 12g   Sat Fat 7g   Salt 0.3g

45g (1½oz) butter
1 teaspoon grated lemon zest
60g (2oz) caster sugar
2 medium eggs
60g (2oz) self-raising flour
70g (2½oz) fresh cherries, stoned and finely chopped
100g (3½oz) dark chocolate, minimum 70% cocoa solids, broken into pieces

Preheat the oven to 180°C/350°F/gas mark 4. Place a 12-hole madeleine tray in the fridge. Melt the butter in a small saucepan, ensuring it doesn't get too hot. When the madeleine tray is cold, brush with a little of the melted butter. As the tray is cold, you will see the butter solidify, showing you that the tray is completely greased. Return to the fridge.

Put the lemon zest, caster sugar and eggs into a medium bowl and mix together. Sift in the flour and mix again, so that everything is evenly combined. Stir in the remaining melted butter and, finally, the chopped cherries. Spoon the mixture into the madeleine tray so that each shell is two-thirds full. Bake for 10 minutes. Turn out onto a wire rack to cool.

Melt the chocolate in a heatproof bowl set over a saucepan of simmering water, ensuring that the bowl doesn't touch the water.

Serve two madeleines per person with the chocolate alongside for dipping.

chocolate, almond and olive oil madeleines

These are not truly madeleines, but were inspired by one I had some time ago in the Michelin-starred Campagne restaurant in Kilkenny, Ireland. Made using ground almonds, it was wonderfully chewy and sticky. The experience stayed with me, so I have tried recreating them. Inspiration also comes from Nigella Lawson, and this is adapted from a cake recipe of hers, which assisted me in my mission. These are almost brownie-like in texture, needing nothing more than a strong coffee to wash them down.

Makes 24/Serves 12

calories 161

V

Carbs 9.5g   Sugar 9g   Protein 4.5g   Fibre 0.5g   Fat 11.5g   Sat Fat 2g   Salt 0.1g

butter, for brushing
35g (1¼oz) cocoa powder, plus extra for dusting
65ml (2½fl oz) boiling water
2 medium eggs
100g (3½oz) caster sugar
70ml (3fl oz) olive oil
125g (4½oz) ground almonds
½ teaspoon baking powder
pinch of sea salt

Place two 12-hole madeleine trays in the fridge. Melt the butter, ensuring it doesn't get too hot, then when the trays are cold, brush with a little of the melted butter. Return to the fridge, and repeat this step once more and then dust the tray with cocoa. Leave in the fridge until needed. Preheat the oven to 170°C/350°F/gas mark 4.

Mix the cocoa with the boiling water to make a smooth paste. Either using a handheld electric whisk or an electric stand mixer, whisk together the eggs, sugar and olive oil for about 5 minutes until pale and thick. Stir in the chocolate paste, followed by the ground almonds, baking powder and pinch of salt, and then mix well.

Pour into the prepared trays and bake for 10 minutes. Be careful here to not overfill each mould; they need to be only half-full to create a perfectly-sized madeleine. When ready, cool for about 5 minutes in the trays and then turn out onto a wire rack to cool completely. Serve two madeleines per person.

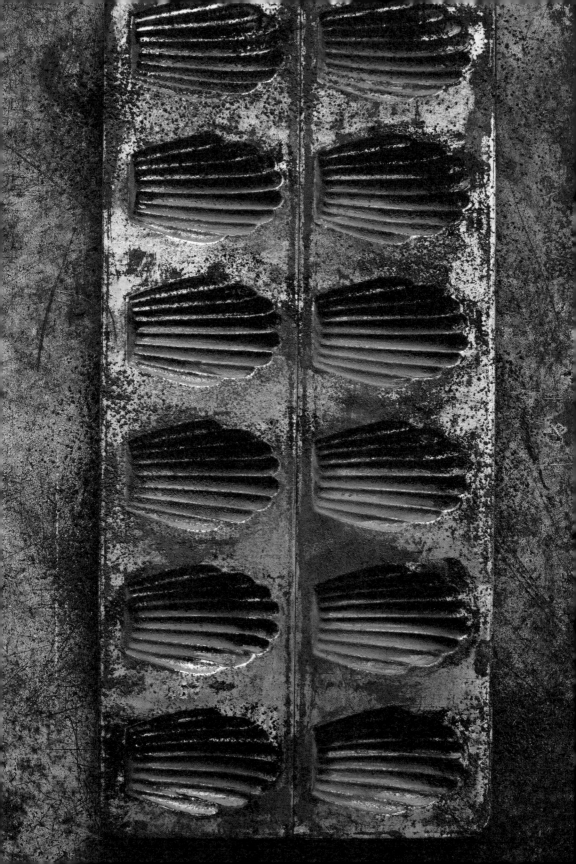

chocolate cherry mousse cake

Although the freezer is used here, this is not served frozen. It simply allows you to set one small sphere inside another. The result looks great!

Serves 10

GF

Carbs 19g   Sugar 19g   Protein 4.5g   Fibre 0.5g   Fat 18g   Sat Fat 11.5g   Salt trace

100g (3½oz) milk chocolate, 40% cocoa solids, broken into pieces

350ml (12fl oz) whipping cream

10 Fabbri Amarena cherries, available from Italian delis or online

250g (9oz) 0% fat Greek yogurt

3 gelatine leaves

75g (2½oz) caster sugar

75ml (2½fl oz) Fabbri Amarena cherry syrup

juice of 1 lemon

1 vanilla pod, halved and seeds scraped out

40g (1½oz) dark chocolate, minimum 70% cocoa solids, melted to decorate

fresh cherries, to serve (optional)

Note: For this, you need a medium and a large spherical mould (also known as a hemisphere cake tin), available in baking shops and online.

Line one 21 x 10cm (8¼ x 4in) and one 16 x 8cm (6¼ x 3in) hemisphere tin with clingfilm, with some over the edges. Ensure to not leave any gaps at all.

Melt the milk chocolate in a heatproof bowl set over a saucepan of simmering water, ensuring the bowl doesn't touch the water. Set aside to cool slightly, but so it is still liquid. Whip 250ml (9fl oz) of the cream to soft peaks, and then pour over the melted chocolate. Fold once with a spatula to create a marbled effect. Pour into the prepared medium tin, press the cherries into the mousse and freeze for about 2 hours, or until set enough to remove from the mould.

Meanwhile, whip the remaining cream until soft peaks form. Beat the yogurt a little with a wooden spoon so that it is smooth and then fold into the cream.

Soak the gelatine in cold water for 5 minutes. Place the caster sugar, cherry syrup, lemon juice, vanilla pod and seeds in a saucepan and boil gently until the sugar has dissolved. Squeeze out the gelatine and whisk into the warm syrup. Cool slightly before folding into the yogurt mixture. Pour into the large spherical mould.

Remove the medium cake from its mould and set into the mousse, pressing down gently so that it is immersed. Freeze for at least 6 hours. Remove from the freezer 45 minutes before serving, unmould and place onto your serving plate. Remove the clingfilm.

Run a clean cloth around the cake to clean up any mess. Drizzle the melted dark chocolate over the top; it will harden quickly as the cake will still be quite cold. Leave at room temperature for 45 minutes until serving.

chocolate meringue brownie

This is all chewy meringue and sticky, oozy, gooey chocolate. If you serve it still warm, the chocolate will be molten; however, it is just as good cold, and is a great make-ahead recipe. Either dark or milk chocolate would work. Try serving it with passion fruit yogurt or natural yogurt and fresh passion fruit.

Serves 12

 calories 278

 V

Carbs 33g   Sugar 27g   Protein 4g   Fibre 1g   Fat 14.5g   Sat Fat 9g   Salt 0.1g

4 medium eggs, separated, plus
  1 large egg
small pinch of salt
220g (8oz) caster sugar
¾ tablespoon cornflour
¼ teaspoon white wine vinegar
180g (6½oz) dark chocolate,
  minimum 70% cocoa solids
140g (5oz) unsalted butter,
  cubed
70g (2½oz) plain flour

Note: A deep baking tray is important here to create height around the edges of the meringue to hold in the chocolate filling. However, this would be just as good free-form. Treat it like a pavlova, ensuring the meringue is only about 2.5cm (1in) deep all over.

Preheat the oven to 150°C/300°F/gas mark 2. Line a 30 x 20 x 5cm (12 x 8 x 2in) loose-based baking tray with greaseproof paper. Place the egg whites and a small pinch of salt in the bowl of an electric stand mixer and whisk until soft peaks form. Add 180g (6½oz) of the sugar, 1 tablespoon at a time. When it has all been added, increase the speed to high and whisk for about 7 minutes. Add the cornflour and vinegar and whisk again for another minute. Using a spatula, scrape the mixture into the tin and spread out evenly, creating a little height all around the edges. Bake for 45 minutes.

About 10–15 minutes before the 45 minutes is up, prepare the brownie filling. Place the chocolate and butter in a heatproof bowl set over a saucepan of simmering water, ensuring the bowl doesn't touch the water. Meanwhile, using an electric stand mixer or handheld electric whisk, whisk the large egg plus the yolks with the remaining 40g (1½oz) sugar until pale and thick. In a slow, steady stream, add the melted chocolate mixture and whisk slowly until incorporated. Sift in the flour and mix everything together.

Remove the meringue from the oven and increase the heat to 160°C/325°F/gas mark 3. Spread the chocolate mixture all over the centre of the meringue and return to the oven. Bake for 15 minutes. Remove from the oven, cool slightly and then slice into twelve.

chocolate mousse cake

This baked mousse cake is made with yogurt in place of the double cream more commonly used for this kind of dessert. It truly is a slice of heaven. Light as a feather, yet as rich as a chocolate pudding can be. It is perfect just as it is, but a spoon of crème fraîche will certainly add a touch of decadence. There is absolutely nothing complicated about this recipe. From the time you start making it, 15 minutes will have it ready to go in the oven.

Serves 12

Carbs 31g   Sugar 31g   Protein 6g   Fibre 1g   Fat 11g   Sat Fat 5.5g   Salt 0.2g

plain flour, for dusting
280g (10oz) dark chocolate, minimum 70% cocoa solids
6 medium egg yolks
160g (5½oz) caster sugar
550g (1lb 4oz) full-fat natural yogurt
4 egg whites

Note: this cake can be served still warm. It will be a little harder to slice, but just as delicious.

Preheat the oven to 150°C/300°F/gas mark 2. Grease and line a 24cm (9½in) round cake tin and dust all over with a little flour. Set aside. (If you are using a spring-form tin, cover the outside of the base and sides thoroughly with three layers of foil to stop water leaking into the tin while baking.)

Place the chocolate in a heatproof bowl set over a saucepan of simmering water, ensuring the water does not touch the bowl. Allow to melt, stirring from time to time. When melted, set aside to cool a little.

Place the egg yolks and half of the sugar in a medium bowl and whisk with a handheld electric whisk until pale and thick. Gradually add the cooled chocolate and then mix in the yogurt.

In another medium bowl, whisk the egg whites until soft peaks form. Add the remaining sugar, a little at a time, and whisk until thick and glossy.

Fold the meringue mixture into the chocolate yogurt mixture. Pour into your prepared tin and place in a large, deep roasting tin. Pour in enough hot water to come three-quarters of the way up the tin. Bake for 50 minutes. When cooked, allow to cool, then chill in the fridge for about 2 hours. Serve as is or with a dollop of half-fat crème fraîche.

chocolate roulade with passion fruit mascarpone

This adaptation of a fool-proof Mary Berry classic has a filling packed with passion fruit and mascarpone cream, taking this roulade up a notch. To lessen the calories even more, use just yogurt and add a little sugar.

Serves 10

 calories 261 GF V

Carbs 30g   Sugar 30g   Protein 7g   Fibre 1g   Fat 12g   Sat Fat 7g   Salt 0.2g

160g (5½oz) dark chocolate, minimum 70% cocoa solids
6 medium eggs, separated
160g (5½oz) caster sugar
pinch of salt
20g (¾oz) cocoa powder
150g (5oz) 0% fat Greek yogurt
100g (3½oz) mascarpone cheese
25g (1oz) clear honey
10g (½oz) icing sugar
seeds of 4 passion fruit
salt

Preheat the oven to 180°C/350°F/gas mark 4. Line a 33 x 23cm (13 x 9in) Swiss roll tin with greaseproof paper.

Place the chocolate in a heatproof bowl set over a saucepan of simmering water, ensuring the bowl doesn't touch the water. Stir occasionally and when melted remove from the heat and allow to cool slightly.

In a large bowl, whisk together the egg yolks and sugar until pale and thick. Stir in the cooled chocolate. Whisk the egg whites with a pinch of salt until soft peaks form, then fold a few spoonfuls into the chocolate mixture and then fold in the rest, working gently so as not to knock out too much air. Be patient – it will come together as you fold it. Sift over the cocoa and gently fold again.

Pour into the prepared tin and bake on the middle shelf of the oven for 20–25 minutes, until firm and a little crispy. When done, place a damp tea towel over the tin and allow to cool. This stops the roulade from drying out too much, which can make it crack when rolling.

Mix the yogurt, mascarpone and honey until smooth. Lay a piece of greaseproof paper on a flat surface and sift over the icing sugar. Gently turn out the roulade and peel away the paper. Spread over the mascarpone, then the passion fruit pulp. Cut a shallow line 2.5cm (1in) from the long edge of the roulade – this makes it easier to fold. Roll tightly, using the paper to help you. It will crack a little, but this is fine. Slice and serve.

rich chocolate fennel cream pots with pomegranate

Some of the greatest things come in small packages, and while these pots are somewhat little, they are totally gorgeous, rich and indulgent. Although the chocolate is infused with fennel, it doesn't actually taste of fennel. This simply gives the chocolate another dimension, making it even more special. However, if fennel is not your thing and you are unsure, simply leave it out.

Serves 6

 calories 276 GF V

Carbs 25g   Sugar 25g   Protein 4.5g   Fibre 1g   Fat 17g   Sat Fat 10g   Salt 0.2g

160g (5½oz) dark chocolate, minimum 70% cocoa solids, broken into pieces

50g (1¾oz) caster sugar

50g (1¾oz) unsalted butter, cubed

1 heaped tablespoon fennel seeds

pinch of sea salt

2 medium eggs, separated

30g (1oz) half-fat crème fraîche

20g (¾oz) fresh pomegranate seeds, to decorate

Tip: if you have used a fresh pomegranate, it is nice to drizzle a little pomegranate juice over the chocolate pots before serving.

Place the chocolate, sugar, butter, fennel seeds and salt in a heatproof bowl with 50ml (1¾fl oz) water. Place over a saucepan of barely simmering water, ensuring the bowl does not touch the water. Melt the chocolate, stirring from time to time. It is important to melt the chocolate as slowly as possible, to allow the maximum time for the fennel flavour to infuse. Once melted, turn off the heat and leave for another 10 minutes. There will be enough steam to keep the chocolate warm while the fennel flavour continues infusing.

When ready, pass the chocolate through a sieve into a medium bowl. Scrape the bottom of the sieve to ensure you have as much of the chocolate as possible and then discard the fennel seeds.

Whisk the egg whites until soft peaks form. Whisk the egg yolks into the chocolate and then fold in the egg whites. Spoon into six 100ml (3½fl oz) glasses or cups and refrigerate until completely set – 2–3 hours or overnight.

To serve, top each with a spoonful of crème fraîche and decorate with fresh pomegranate seeds.

popcorn and caramel éclairs

This recipe is the epitome of utter indulgence without any sacrifice. There are a few steps to go through, but you won't be sorry you took the time!

Makes 12

calories
190

V

Carbs 19g   Sugar 8.5g   Protein 7g   Fibre 1g   Fat 9g   Sat Fat 5g   Salt 0.4g

75ml (2½fl oz) semi-skimmed milk

70g (2½oz) unsalted butter, cubed

20g (1oz) caster sugar

pinch of salt

seeds of 1 vanilla pod

150g (5oz) plain flour

3 medium eggs

20g (¾oz) popping corn

1 teaspoon sunflower oil

15g (½oz) peanut butter

15g (½oz) maple syrup (honey will also work here)

½ teaspoon Maldon sea salt

250g (9oz) 0% fat Greek yogurt

40g (1½oz) caramel

70g (2½oz) dark chocolate, minimum 70% cocoa solids, melted

Note: you can store unfilled éclairs in an airtight container, then fill and decorate just before serving. The éclairs will keep for a few days.

Preheat the oven to 180°C/350°F/gas mark 4. Line two large and one small baking tray with greaseproof paper.

Put the milk, butter, half the sugar, salt, vanilla seeds and 125ml (4fl oz) of water in a saucepan over a medium heat. Sift the flour onto a sheet of greaseproof paper. When the butter has melted, pour in the flour. Beat with a wooden spoon, over the heat, until a smooth dough forms that comes away from the edges.

Transfer the dough to an electric mixer and beat for 1–2 minutes to cool. Once cool, add the eggs, one at a time, beating constantly, ensuring each is fully incorporated. Transfer to a piping bag and pipe twelve éclairs onto the large baking trays, each about 12cm (4½in) long. Bake for 25 minutes until golden and hollow.

Place the popping corn in a saucepan with the sunflower oil over a medium heat. Cover with a lid and shake from time to time until all the corn has popped. In a bowl, mix together the peanut butter, maple syrup and salt until smooth. Add the popcorn and toss to coat. Transfer to the small baking tray and bake for 5 minutes to crisp, turning halfway through. Set aside.

Mix the yogurt, remaining sugar and caramel until smooth. Transfer to a piping bag and chill until needed.

Transfer the cooked éclairs to a wire rack and when cool enough to handle, pierce a small hole in the end of each one.

When cold, pipe in the yogurt mixture, drizzle over the melted chocolate and sprinkle with the popcorn. Leave to set, then serve.

white chocolate rice pudding with vanilla honey figs

This is not the kind of dessert that springs to mind when you think of low calorie. In short, it's not. However, in this recipe I have opted to use semi-skimmed milk and light evaporated milk which work perfectly. The rice expands so much and absorbs so much liquid, that you actually don't need a huge quantity. All of these tweaks help to bring the calorie content down significantly. But as you can see, it looks just as good as it should!

Serves 6

 calories 238 GF V

Carbs 37g   Sugar 24g   Protein 8g   Fibre 1g   Fat 6g   Sat Fat 3.5g   Salt 0.2g

100g (3½oz) pudding rice
300ml (10fl oz) light
   evaporated milk
400ml (14fl oz) semi-skimmed
   milk
50g (1¾oz) white chocolate,
   grated
20g (¾oz) caster sugar
2 vanilla pods, halved and
   seeds scraped out
4 medium fresh figs
40g (1½oz) clear honey

Preheat the oven to 150°C/300°F/gas mark 2. Place the rice, milks, white chocolate, caster sugar and one vanilla pod with its seeds in a baking dish. Stir to combine and bake in the oven for 1 hour. Stir from time to time, ensuring the rice is evenly distributed and not sticking together in large clumps.

Prepare the figs. Slice a deep cross into the top of each one and squeeze the fruit so that it opens a little at the top, exposing the flesh. Mix the honey with the remaining vanilla seeds and set aside.

After 1 hour, remove the rice pudding from the oven. Stir one more time, then place the figs into the rice, cut side up, and pour the honey all over each one. Cook for a further 30 minutes and, when ready, serve immediately.

white chocolate, blueberry and lemon jellies

This is simple to execute, but takes some time and a little patience. The end result is visually gorgeous though. The chocolate is sweet, the blueberry is fragrant and the lemon deliberately tart to cut through and create balance.

Serves 6

 calories 103 GF

Carbs 19g   Sugar 19g   Protein 1.5g   Fibre 0g   Fat 2.5g   Sat Fat 1.5g   Salt trace

sunflower oil, for greasing
250ml (9fl oz) concentrated
   blueberry juice
20g (¾oz) clear honey
1 vanilla pod, halved
5 gelatine leaves
40g (1½oz) white chocolate
200ml (7fl oz) unsweetened
   almond milk
grated zest of 1 lemon and
   juice of 2
50g (1¾oz) sugar
50ml (2fl oz) water

Note: to create the layered effect shown opposite, the process is the same but it takes more time. Just make sure to allow enough time to chill each layer to ensure it sets.

Grease six 100ml (3½fl oz) dariole moulds with a tiny bit of sunflower oil on some kitchen paper. Set aside.

Place the blueberry juice, honey and half the vanilla pod with its seeds in a saucepan and gently warm for 5 minutes. Soak 2 leaves of gelatine in cold water for 5 minutes. Allow to cool for a few minutes, then whisk in the squeezed gelatine. Divide between the moulds and refrigerate for about 2 hours until set.

Melt the white chocolate in a heatproof bowl set over a saucepan of simmering water, ensuring it does not touch the water, stirring occasionally. Soak 1½ of the gelatine leaves in cold water for 5 minutes. In a separate saucepan, heat the almond milk with the remaining half vanilla pod and its seeds. Remove the chocolate from the heat and slowly whisk in the almond milk then the squeezed gelatine. Cool a little, divide between the moulds and refrigerate until set.

Heat the lemon zest and juice, sugar and water in a small saucepan, stirring from time to time, until the sugar has dissolved. Soak the remaining 1½ gelatine leaves as before and, when ready, whisk into the lemon liquid. Divide between the dariole moulds and return to the refrigerator until set again.

To serve, dip the moulds into hot water for 1–2 seconds and turn each upside down onto a small plate.

white chocolate, melon and mint fruit salad

This dessert is uncomplicated – nothing more than a marriage of delicious, refreshing flavours.

Serves 4

GF   V

Carbs 48g   Sugar 48g   Protein 3.5g   Fibre 4g   Fat 8g   Sat Fat 4.5g   Salt 0.1g

100g (3½oz) caster sugar
generous handful of mint,
   leaves picked, plus 3 extra
   sprigs for the syrup
900g (2lb) cantaloupe melon,
   deseeded (or use mixed
   varieties for interest)
100g (3½oz) white chocolate,
   broken into pieces

Place the sugar in a medium saucepan with 100ml (3½fl oz) water and three sprigs of mint. Bring to a gentle simmer and cook until the sugar has completely dissolved, stirring from time to time. Set aside to cool and then remove the mint.

Using a melon baller, scoop out the flesh of the melon. Alternatively, slice into 2cm (¾in) chunks.

Melt the chocolate in a heatproof bowl set over a saucepan of simmering water, ensuring the bowl does not touch the water, and then spread out thinly on a large, flat, clean baking tray. Allow to cool and harden, and then peel away curls of the chocolate using the back of a knife.

Arrange the melon on a large serving platter, pour over the syrup, scatter with the remaining mint leaves and decorate with the white chocolate curls.

white chocolate crème brûlée

Jersey milk is used here in the absence of cream; it is just that
bit creamier and richer than plain whole milk, and so makes for
a better substitute. However, I have also made this brûlée with
everyday whole milk, which also works a treat if you can't
find the Jersey variety.

Serves 4

 calories 281 GF V

Carbs 32g   Sugar 27g   Protein 8g   Fibre 0g   Fat 13g   Sat Fat 6g   Salt 2g

350ml (12fl oz) whole Jersey
  milk
150ml (5fl oz) semi-skimmed
  milk
50g (1¾oz) white chocolate,
  finely chopped
1 vanilla pod, halved and
  seeds scraped out
4 egg yolks
1½ tablespoons cornflour
40g (1½oz) clear honey
30g (1oz) caster sugar

Preheat the oven to 150°C/300°F/gas mark 2.
Place four ramekins in a roasting tin deep enough
to allow you to pour water halfway up the sides of
them (creating a bain-marie).

Place the milks, chocolate and vanilla pod and seeds
in a medium saucepan and slowly heat until it is just
below boiling point. When ready, in a heatproof bowl,
whisk together the egg yolks, cornflour and honey
until combined.

In a slow, steady stream, add the hot milk to the
egg yolk mixture, stirring constantly. Pass through
a sieve into a jug, and then pour the custard into
the ramekins.

Pour hot water into the tray, ensuring it comes halfway
up the sides of the ramekins. Bake for 35 minutes.
The brûlées should still have a bit of a wobble when
you take them out of the oven. Chill thoroughly in
the fridge for about an hour.

Sprinkle some sugar all over the top of each one and,
using a blow torch, caramelize the sugar. Allow to cool
before serving but don't refrigerate.

sicilian watermelon pudding

This watermelon pudding (known as *gelo di melone*) is native to Palermo, Sicily. Armed with a nice ripe watermelon, this dessert captures its flavour beautifully. Served with lots of grated chocolate and pistachios, it's often flavoured with jasmine, which I feel is too floral. Avoid the temptation to buy the smaller baby watermelons often available in supermarkets, as they never have much flavour. Go for a bigger one, and use any leftovers to make granita, or blitz and use the juice for summer spritzers.

Serves 4

Carbs 40g   Sugar 31g   Protein 3g   Fibre 0.5g   Fat 7.5g   Sat Fat 3g   Salt trace

600g (1lb 5oz) peeled watermelon (prepared weight)

40g (1½oz) cornflour

50g (1¾oz) caster sugar, or more to taste

juice of ½ lime, or more to taste

40g (1½oz) dark chocolate, minimum 70% cocoa solids, finely chopped

15g (½oz) white chocolate, finely chopped

25g (1oz) pistachio nibs (or shelled pistachios, chopped)

Using a handheld blender, blitz the watermelon in a medium bowl until smooth. Pass through a sieve and pour into a medium saucepan over a low heat. Allow the watermelon to infuse for about 5 minutes and then pass through a sieve again.

In another medium bowl, mix together the cornflour, sugar, lime juice and about 100ml (3½fl oz) of the watermelon juice to form a smooth paste. Add the rest of the juice and then return to the saucepan and place over a medium heat. Bring to the boil and cook for about 5–7 minutes, stirring constantly. The mixture will start to thicken and will become a watermelon red colour again (it will have turned cloudy pink with the addition of cornflour). Taste to ensure the flavour of cornflour has been cooked off, and add a touch more sugar or lime juice as needed.

Remove from the heat and cover with clingfilm to prevent a skin forming, then allow to cool to room temperature. Transfer to clear serving glasses and refrigerate until totally chilled and set.

Before serving, decorate with the chocolate and pistachio nibs.

fruit

This chapter champions all that seasonal fruit has to offer, and aims to keep it simple in order to let each individual fruit shine. Seasonality is so important here. We have lost the concept of seasons — indeed some of us never even had it — through no fault of our own, but simply through the year-round availability of fruit. It may not seem necessary to eat seasonally when we can get our hands on strawberries in the middle of February, however, I urge you to eat the fruit our seasons offer us; it is simply so much better, tasting just how it should. If you only ever ate a strawberry in February, you would never truly know what a strawberry should taste like, which is a very simple and humble pleasure offered to us by nature.

Speaking of which, strawberries take centre stage in the Strawberry Soufflé, which is light, delicate and simply delicious. A buttermilk panna cotta is infused with fragrant toasted almonds and very simply teamed with ripe plums and grappa. This flavour combination is an absolute winner. In another recipe, plump peaches are soaked in a syrup of lemon, vanilla and Sauternes — a dollop of crème fraîche and a scattering of pecan nuts are all that's required to make it a perfect dessert. For a showstopper, boozy rum-soaked babas and delicate apricots bring out the best in one another, and I would serve this for a special occasion, because this dessert really is something special. I think the flavours of rum, thyme and apricots were made for each other. Speaking of showstoppers, the Mango, Blueberry and Coconut Cheesecake is a feast for the eyes with a layer of vibrant yellow mango set above a creamy cheesecake base.

Once again, a few traditional desserts find their way into this chapter. One in the form of a crumble and the other a delicious summer pudding. Both have a few interesting twists to make them fresh and new, and of course, lower in calories, as well as, most notably, the aptly named Who Needs Bread and Butter? Turn to page 84 if you love bread and butter pudding — this is your low-calorie answer.

almond buttermilk panna cotta with plums and grappa

A panna cotta made with buttermilk is significantly lighter than one made just with cream. You can use shop-bought flaked almonds for this recipe, but I would recommend toasting your own. The flavour will be fresher and more intense. Always toast nuts in a dry frying pan and watch them closely as they burn quickly.

Serves 6

 calories 174 GF

Carbs 16.5g   Sugar 16.5g   Protein 5g   Fibre 0.5g   Fat 8.5g   Sat Fat 4.5g   Salt 0.2g

400ml (14fl oz) buttermilk
200ml (7fl oz) single cream
20g (¾oz) flaked almonds, toasted
60g (2oz) caster sugar
3 gelatine leaves
3 ripe plums, mixed varieties if possible
45ml (1½ fl oz) grappa

Place the buttermilk, cream, toasted flaked almonds and sugar in a saucepan and heat for about 5 minutes until it is just below simmering point. Do not boil the mixture as it will separate. Remove from the heat and leave for about 10 minutes to infuse. Meanwhile, place the gelatine in a bowl of cold water and leave to soak for 5 minutes.

Strain the buttermilk mixture into a clean saucepan and heat again without boiling. When hot, squeeze the water out of the gelatine and whisk it through the liquid.

Pour into six panna cotta moulds and refrigerate until set. I tend to make panna cotta either the night before or the morning of the evening I am going to serve them. You want to ensure they have enough time to fully set. Quarter and stone the plums and mix with the grappa. Leave to infuse until the panna cotta are ready.

When ready to serve, dip the moulds very briefly into a bowl of hot water and turn each upside down onto a plate or bowl. Tap gently if they are a bit stubborn. Serve with the grappa-soaked plums.

berries, tarragon honey and sablé biscuits

Often the flavour of herbs can marry beautifully with fruit. The very gentle aniseed aroma of tarragon really makes this very simple berry dessert something more special. Ensure you thoroughly wash the berries and set aside to dry before making these.

Serves 4

 calories 87

Carbs 11.5g   Sugar 7.5g   Protein 1g   Fibre 1g   Fat 4g   Sat Fat 2.5g   Salt trace

80g (3oz) honey
2 sprigs of tarragon
300g (7oz) blackberries
300g (7oz) blueberries
60ml (2½fl oz) single cream

For the sablé biscuits
70g (2½oz) unsalted butter, cubed
100g (3½oz) plain flour
50g (1¾oz) icing sugar
pinch of sea salt flakes
1 medium egg yolk
1 teaspoon vanilla bean paste

Note: Each portion is two biscuits, but you will have some left over. They are a delicious afternoon treat, served with tea or coffee. Simply keep in an airtight container and enjoy at your leisure!

Place the honey and tarragon in a small saucepan, bring to the boil, remove from the heat and allow to infuse while you make the biscuits.

Rub the butter into the flour and icing sugar until it resembles fine breadcrumbs. Alternatively, this can be done in a food-processor. Add the salt and mix well. Whisk the egg yolk with the vanilla bean paste and add to the mixture. Bring together with your hands and knead lightly until you have a smooth dough.

Roll into a log about 15 x 2.5cm (6 x 1in). Wrap tightly in clingfilm. Refrigerate for at least 30 minutes (this step can also be done in advance).

When ready to cook, preheat the oven to 180°C/350°F/ gas mark 4. Line a large baking tray with greaseproof paper. Remove the clingfilm from the dough and slice into small biscuits, each one about 5mm (¼in) thick. Place onto the lined baking tray and bake for 7–10 minutes until they are golden brown.

Toss the berries in the tarragon honey. Serve with a drizzle of cream and two sablé biscuits each.

gooseberry and blackberry pudding

A traditional summer pudding gets a bit of a makeover here with the addition of gooseberries. They are so underused, and I adore them. They add a gorgeous sourness to this sometimes oversweet pudding. Wash the fruit and discard any that are damaged before you start this recipe.

Serves 6

 calories 231 DF V

Carbs 45g   Sugar 23g   Protein 6g   Fibre 7g   Fat 1.5g   Sat Fat 0g   Salt 0.5g

450g (1lb) blackberries
200g (7oz) gooseberries
200g (7oz) raspberries
80g (3oz) caster sugar
juice of ½ orange
7–8 slices good-quality white
   bloomer bread
single cream, to serve
   (optional)

Place all the fruit in a saucepan with the sugar and orange juice. Very gently stir everything together and simmer for about 4 minutes, until the fruit starts to give up its juice and soften slightly. Remove from the heat, and strain the juices off into a bowl.

Slice the crusts from the bread. Using an 850ml (1½ pint) pudding bowl as a guide, cut out a circle of bread to fit onto the top of the pudding. Line the bowl with two large sheets of clingfilm, ensuring that some is left hanging over the side. Dip each remaining slice of bread in the warm fruit juices and line the pudding bowl, overlapping the bread tightly as you go and ensuring there are no gaps.

Pour in the fruit, and finish with the remaining circle of bread. Reheat the remaining juice, pour all over and cover with the over-hanging clingfilm. Place a plate on top and weigh down with something heavy. Refrigerate overnight.

When ready to serve, tip the pudding out onto a serving plate, remove the clingfilm, slice and serve with fresh cream, if using.

blueberry, lemon and vanilla crumble

I grew up eating crumble. Apples and rhubarb grew in our garden and my
mum was a dab hand at this humble, satisfying dessert. She would throw a
handful of cornflakes into her topping to add both crunch and chewiness.
Couldn't be better! This is delicious served with cream or yogurt, but the
blueberries give so much juice that nothing extra is actually required.

Serves 6

 calories 276 V

Carbs 46g · Sugar 26g · Protein 4g · Fibre 3g · Fat 8g · Sat Fat 4.5g · Salt 0.2g

700g (1lb 9oz) frozen
  blueberries
60g (2oz) clear honey
zest of 1 lemon and juice of ½
1 vanilla pod, halved and seeds
  scraped out

For the topping
50g (1¾oz) butter, cubed
100g (3½oz) plain flour
50g (1¾oz) soft light brown
  sugar
40g (1½oz) jumbo porridge
  oats
25g (1oz) cornflakes

Preheat the oven to 180°C/350°F/gas mark 4. Mix
together the blueberries, honey, lemon zest and juice
and vanilla pod and seeds and pour into a baking dish
roughly 25 x 15cm (10 x 6in). Set aside.

For the topping, rub the butter into the flour and
sugar until it resembles breadcrumbs (alternatively
do this in a food-processor). Stir in the porridge oats
and cornflakes. Scatter all over the top of the blueberry
mixture and bake for 30–35 minutes, or until golden
brown all over and bubbling underneath.

Serve with ice cream, custard, Greek yogurt or double
cream, if you wish.

coffee and blackberry millefeuille

Wafer thin layers of crispy pastry drenched in a maple chestnut glaze and filled with a punchy coffee cream and tart blackberries — the perfect late summer into autumn dessert.

Makes 6

calories 237

V

Carbs 17g   Sugar 6.5g   Protein 3g   Fibre 1.5g   Fat 17g   Sat Fat 10g   Salt 0.3g

plain flour, for dusting
160g (5½oz) ready-rolled puff pastry (½ 320g/11oz packet)
3 tablespoons ground coffee
4 tablespoons boiling water
100g (2oz) soft ricotta
10g (½oz) caster sugar
100ml (3½fl oz) double cream
30g (1oz) maple syrup
50g (1¾oz) chestnut purée
100g (3½oz) blackberries, halved

Preheat the oven to 180°C/350°F/gas mark 4. Have ready two large baking trays and two large pieces of greaseproof paper.

Flour a flat surface and a rolling pin. Roll the pastry out until it is 40cm (16in) long. Sandwich between the pieces of greaseproof paper on one baking tray, and weigh down with the other baking tray on top. Bake for about 10 minutes, or until golden brown and crisp. When ready, remove from the oven and allow to cool.

Meanwhile, prepare the coffee cream. Mix the ground coffee and boiling water together and leave to infuse for a few minutes. Strain through a cheesecloth, muslin or clean tea towel into a jug, squeezing out as much of the liquid as possible.

Mix together the ricotta and sugar until smooth, then stir in the coffee. Whip the cream until soft peaks form and then fold through the ricotta mixture. Transfer to a piping bag fitted with a small round nozzle and refrigerate until needed. Mix together the maple syrup and chestnut purée and set aside.

Trim the edges of the pastry and cut it into 20 rectangles, roughly 10 x 5cm (4 x 2in). You will have 20 pieces but only need 18, so use the best ones. To assemble, place 6 blackberries on a sheet of pastry and pipe cream in between. Top with more pastry and repeat. Place a final sheet of pastry on top and spread over a thin layer of the glaze. Repeat and serve immediately.

exotic fruit jelly

This dessert is as pretty as a painting — a definite showstopper.
Slice with a very sharp knife and if you would like to serve it with
something, some coconut yogurt would be perfect. You can use
different fruits here, but steer clear of pineapple and kiwi,
as they will prevent the jelly from setting properly.

Serves 10

· ·

Carbs 11.6g   Sugar 11.6g   Protein 1.3g   Fibre 0.1g   Fat 0.3g   Sat Fat 0.2g   Salt 0.2g

· ·

9 gelatine leaves
50ml (2fl oz) white rum
juice of 2 limes
50g (1¾oz) caster sugar
750ml (25 fl oz) coconut water
1 ripe mango, peeled, stoned
    and cut into 1cm (½in) cubes
1 star fruit, thinly sliced
1 dragon fruit, flesh cubed
100g (3½oz) strawberries,
    thinly sliced
4 sprigs of mint, leaves picked

Soak the gelatine leaves in a large bowl of cold water
for 5 minutes, ensuring they don't clump together
(this will stop them from dissolving properly). Place
the rum, lime juice and sugar in a small saucepan and
heat to just below boiling point. Remove the gelatine
from the water and squeeze out as much excess water
as possible. Whisk into the heated liquid until totally
dissolved.

Transfer to a large bowl and stir in the coconut water.
Place in the fridge and busy yourself with something
that keeps you in the kitchen, as it needs to be checked
every 15 minutes for about 1 hour while it begins to set.
It is important to watch it closely, as you want it at the
stage where it is thick enough to hold the fruit but not
so thick that it becomes lumpy when stirred.

When ready, set aside 150ml (5fl oz) of the jelly.
Pour one third of the remaining jelly into a 1-litre
(1¾-pint) jelly mould and add one third of the
mixed fruit and mint leaves, arranging them evenly
and carefully. Repeat until you have used all of the fruit
and mint leaves and then cover with the reserved jelly.

Refrigerate for 5–6 hours, or overnight, until set.
When ready to serve, simply release the edges of the
jelly with your fingers or a blunt knife, turn upside
down onto a serving plate and tap to release.

mango cheesecake with toasted coconut

I personally am not a fan of cheesecakes that are dense and heavy.
This is anything but: on the contrary, it is as light as a feather.

Serves 10

calories
246

Carbs 30.4g Sugar 21.6g Protein 8.8g Fibre 1.6g Fat 9.6g Sat Fat 5.2g Salt 0.4g

150g (5oz) ginger nut biscuits
30g (1oz) butter, melted
5g (⅛–¼oz) fresh ginger,
   peeled and grated (about
   ½ teaspoon)
125g (4½oz) golden caster
   sugar
200g (7oz) light cream cheese
280g (10oz) 0% fat Greek
   yogurt
3 medium eggs, separated
grated zest and juice of 1 lime
1 tablespoon cornflour
2 medium ripe mangoes,
   peeled, stoned and flesh
   removed
juice of 1 lemon
3 gelatine leaves, soaked in
   cold water for 5 minutes,
   then squeezed to remove
   any excess water
10g (½oz) dried coconut flakes
20g (¾oz) blueberries

Preheat the oven to 180°C/350°F/gas mark 4. Grease
and line a 20cm (8in) round spring-form tin. Place
the biscuits in a food-processor and blitz until they
resemble fine breadcrumbs. (Alternatively, put them
in a sealed plastic bag and crush using a rolling pin.)
Add the melted butter and ginger and mix to combine.
Tip into the prepared tin and press firmly down over
the base to create an even layer. Bake for 5 minutes.

In the bowl of an electric stand mixer, beat together
half of the sugar with the cream cheese, yogurt, egg
yolks, lime zest and juice and cornflour. In a separate
bowl, whisk the egg whites until soft peaks form. Add
the remaining sugar, a little at a time, and whisk for
about 4 minutes until thick and glossy. Gently fold one
third of the egg whites into the cream cheese mixture.
When incorporated, fold in the rest. Pour this over the
base, and then bake on the middle shelf of the oven for
50 minutes. Allow to cool completely in the tin, and
chill overnight if possible. Trim it slightly if necessary
so that the surface is relatively flat.

Blitz the mango flesh with 100ml (3½fl oz) water until
smooth; you want to end up with approximately 350g
(12oz) purée. Heat the lemon juice in a small saucepan
until almost boiling. Add the squeezed gelatine and
whisk to melt. Stir into the mango purée and then
pour over the cheesecake. Chill in the fridge for at
least 4 hours to set.

Toast the coconut in a dry frying pan, cool, then use
it decorate the cheesecake along with the blueberries.

old fashioned

Based on the cocktail of the same name, this dessert is definitely a boozy one, but the alcohol is balanced by a mound of juicy orange segments. This is the perfect party dessert choice!

Serves 6

 calories 89   DF   GF

Carbs 14g   Sugar 14g   Protein 1g   Fibre 0.5g   Fat 0g   Sat Fat 0g   Salt trace

50g (1¾oz) caster sugar
1 teaspoon angostura bitters
75ml (2½fl oz) bourbon
100ml (3½fl oz) orange juice
    (from 2 medium or 1 large
    oranges)
4 gelatine leaves
400ml (14fl oz) soda water
2 oranges, peeled and
    segmented

Place the sugar, angostura bitters, bourbon and orange juice in a small saucepan and heat to dissolve the sugar, stirring from time to time.

Soak the gelatine leaves in a bowl of cold water for at least 5 minutes. Once they have been soaking for a couple of minutes, ensure to separate them, as they clump together and cause lumps when added to the hot liquid.

When ready, squeeze the gelatine leaves to remove excess water and then whisk into the hot bourbon mixture. Stir in the soda water and gently mix everything together – you want to keep as much fizz as possible. Pour into six glasses and refrigerate until set.

Just before serving, pile some fresh orange segments on top of each glass.

strawberry soufflés

Soufflés seem like a daunting dessert to tackle, but the truth is that the prep
is the easiest bit. If you can nail this, then the rest should be plain sailing.
An oven thermometer helps as the correct oven temperature will certainly
help things along. Have a go. Even if something goes wrong along the way
and they don't come out of the oven perfect, the mixture tastes dreamy,
so you won't go hungry!

Makes 6

calories 264 V

Carbs 30g   Sugar 27g   Protein 4.5g   Fibre 3.5g   Fat 13g   Sat Fat 7g   Salt 0.1g

150ml (5fl oz) milk
100ml (3½fl oz) double cream
1 vanilla pod, halved and seeds
   scraped out
3 medium egg yolks
125g (4½oz) caster sugar
15g (½oz) plain flour
10g (½oz) cornflour
500g (18oz) strawberries,
   hulled and washed
butter, for greasing
2 egg whites

Heat the milk, cream and vanilla pod and seeds in a
medium saucepan until it is just before boiling point.

Whisk the egg yolks and 40g (1½oz) of the sugar together
until pale and thick. Whisk in the flour and cornflour.
Remove the vanilla pods from the milk and gradually
whisk the liquid into the egg mixture. Return to the
saucepan and heat gently, whisking constantly for about
10 minutes, until smooth and thick. Transfer to
a bowl, and lay a sheet of clingfilm on top of the custard
so that a skin doesn't form. Allow to cool completely.

Meanwhile, blitz the strawberries with 20g (¾oz) of
the remaining sugar and pass through a very fine sieve
to remove any seeds. Transfer to a saucepan and boil
for 15 minutes, until reduced by half. Allow to cool.

Grease six 200ml (7fl oz) ramekins with a little bit of
butter and then dust all over with 15g (½oz) of the sugar.

When you are ready to make the soufflés, preheat the
oven to 190°C/375°F/gas mark 5. Mix the strawberry
purée with the custard base. In a separate bowl, whisk the
egg whites until soft peaks form. Whisk in the remaining
50g (1¾oz) of the sugar until thick and glossy. Gently
fold into the strawberry mixture. Divide between the
prepared moulds on a baking tray, ensuring they are
three-quarters full. Bake for 17–20 minutes, until
risen and slightly golden. Serve immediately.

peaches in sauternes with crème fraîche and pecans

It is imperative to use best-quality, unbruised, fresh, ripe peaches for this recipe. The leftover syrup is delicious used in cocktails, or frozen to make a boozy ice lolly or granita.

Serves 6

calories 220 · DF · V

Carbs 10g   Sugar 9.5g   Protein 3g   Fibre 2.5g   Fat 18g   Sat Fat 7.5g   Salt trace

250g (9oz) caster sugar
pared rind of 1 lemon
1 vanilla pod, halved and seeds scraped out
375ml (13fl oz) Sauternes wine
5 medium ripe peaches, sliced into wedges
150g (5oz) crème fraîche
70g (2½oz) pecans, roughly chopped

Place the sugar, lemon rind and vanilla pod and seeds in a medium saucepan over a medium heat and simmer until the sugar is totally dissolved. Allow to cool completely and then stir in the Sauternes.

Place the peach wedges in a large, clean jar and pour the syrup all over. Cover and leave overnight for the flavours to infuse.

Serve the peaches and juice with a dollop of best-quality crème fraîche and finish with a few chopped pecans.

rum babas with thyme and apricots

Rum, apricots and thyme together are magical. The thyme takes the edge off the rum, while adding an unexpected layer of flavour. Both also serve to bring out the best of fresh apricots. The whole combination is perfection.

Serves 6

Carbs 31g   Sugar 15g   Protein 4g   Fibre 1g   Fat 4.5g   Sat Fat 2.5g   Salt 0.2g

60ml (2½fl oz) semi-skimmed
  milk
125g (4½oz) plain flour
10g (½oz) caster sugar
½ 7g (¼oz) sachet fast-action
  dried yeast
1 medium egg
pinch of salt
25g (1oz) unsalted butter,
  melted
3 fresh ripe apricots, stoned
  and cut into wedges

For the syrup
195g (6¾oz) sugar
4 sprigs of fresh thyme
100ml (3½fl oz) rum

Warm the milk in a small saucepan over a medium heat. Sift the flour and sugar into a bowl and stir through the yeast. Whisk the egg and add the warmed milk and a pinch of salt. Pour into the flour and stir to combine. Add the melted butter and beat everything together until glossy. Cover and set aside in a warm place for about 30 minutes, or until doubled in volume.

Meanwhile, prepare the syrup. Place 270ml (9¼fl oz) water with the sugar and thyme in a medium saucepan and over a medium heat. Stir from time to time, until the sugar has dissolved and the liquid is clear. Boil for 3–4 minutes then remove from the heat. When cooled a little, add the rum. If you want the syrup to taste less boozy, add the alcohol when you start to boil the syrup to eliminate some of the alcohol. Set aside to cool.

When the dough has doubled in size, gently knock it back using a metal spoon. Normally you would do this by hand, but the dough will still be quite sticky. With the same spoon, scoop the dough into a 12-hole silicone baba mould. Cover and place on a tray in a warm place for 30 minutes for the dough to double in size again.

Preheat the oven to 190°C/375°F/gas mark 5. Bake the babas for 10–15 minutes, or until golden brown.

When ready, remove from their moulds and allow to cool on a wire rack. To serve, pierce them a few times with a skewer or fork. Pour the syrup all over and soak for about 5 minutes. When ready, serve with fresh apricots and a tablespoon of syrup.

who needs bread and butter?

This was made with bread and butter pudding in mind, but uses neither of those ingredients. This is the ultimate low calorie alternative — lacking absolutely none of the indulgence. It is based on the sponge cake used for the layered sponge cake on page 37, but flavoured with zesty lime and coconut, then baked in a luscious coconut passion fruit custard. Perfection!

Serves 8

 calories 295 V

Carbs 21g   Sugar 20g   Protein 8g   Fibre 1g   Fat 15g   Sat Fat 9g   Salt 0.5g

110g (4oz) caster sugar
4 medium eggs
grated zest of 2 limes
115g (4oz) self-raising flour
I teaspoon baking powder
20g (¾oz) dried flaked
   coconut, chopped roughly

For the coconut custard
100ml (3½fl oz) double cream
50ml (2fl oz) single cream
150ml (5fl oz) light coconut
   milk
2 medium eggs
40g (1½oz) caster sugar
2 passion fruit, seeds and flesh
   removed

Preheat the oven to 180°C/350°F/gas mark 4. Grease and line a 30 x 20cm (12 x 8in) Swiss roll tin. Place the sugar, eggs and lime zest in the bowl of an electric stand mixer and whisk on a high speed for about 7 minutes until tripled in size, pale in colour, thick and glossy.

Meanwhile, sift together the flour and baking powder in a bowl. Sift into the whisked egg mixture. Using a balloon whisk, scoop up the mixture, and allow it to fall back into the bowl, gently tapping on the bowl if necessary. Very gently repeat this process until all of the flour is incorporated. The aim is to avoid knocking out any of the air, so gentle movements and patience are required. Fold in the flaked coconut.

Scrape the cake mixture evenly into the prepared tin, using a rubber spatula. Bake for 25 minutes. When ready, cool in the tin.

To make the custard, heat the creams and coconut milk in a medium saucepan until hot. Whisk the eggs and sugar together until pale, thick and doubled in size, then gradually add the hot cream, stirring it all the time to prevent the eggs curdling. Set aside.

Cut the sponge into small triangles so that they resemble slices of bread. Lay them in a baking dish, overlapping them as you go. Pour the custard all over, top with the passion fruit, and bake for 25–30 minutes, until risen and golden brown. This is best served warm out of the oven.

lemon grapefruit possets

I was desperate to include a posset recipe in this book. It is one of my all-time favourite desserts and beyond simple to make. However, it is not kind when it comes to calories. I tried it with crème fraîche and with yogurt; all kinds of experiments took place to reduce the calorie count. But without cream, it is simply not a posset, and I came to the valid conclusion that I would rather include it in all of its glory rather than jeopardize its integrity. Yes, the portions are smaller, but it is a very rich dessert, so actually, when I am not being greedy, this size is just right! These are best served in small dessert wine glasses.

Makes 6

 calories 238 GF

Carbs 18g   Sugar 18g   Protein 1g   Fibre 0g   Fat 18g   Sat Fat 11g   Salt trace

85g (3oz) caster sugar
200ml (7fl oz) double cream
grated zest of 1 grapefruit
2 sprigs of mint
juice of 1½ lemons
2 gelatine leaves
250ml (9fl oz) grapefruit juice

Note: complete the first two steps of this recipe the night before you want to serve them. Finish them off the following morning so that they are totally set when ready to serve that evening.

Place 60g (2oz) of the caster sugar with the cream, grapefruit zest and mint in a small saucepan and place over a medium heat. Stir until the sugar dissolves and the mixture has started to bubble around the edges.

Pass through a sieve into a bowl and add the lemon juice, stirring as you do so. The posset will thicken immediately. Pour into six small glasses and refrigerate for 5–6 hours until set.

Soak the gelatine in some cold water for at least 5 minutes. Place the grapefruit juice and remaining 25g (1oz) of the sugar in a small saucepan and heat until the sugar has dissolved. Remove from the heat. Squeeze any excess water from the gelatine and stir into the hot grapefruit juice. Allow to cool for about 10 minutes until just above room temperature; you don't want the mixture to start setting but equally you don't want it to be so hot that it melts the posset when you pour it on top.

When ready, gently pour onto the set possets. Refrigerate once more for 3–4 hours and serve when set.

pomegranate-roasted red grapes, labneh and pistachios

I adore everything about this dessert — creamy labneh, sweet and sour grapes, crunchy pistachios. It has the perfect amount of sweetness to round off any meal, or just for a treat whenever the mood takes you. You need to start preparing the labneh a day ahead, but all this requires is spooning some yogurt into cheesecloth. Pretty simple!

Serves 6   calories 257   GF   V

Carbs 38g   Sugar 37g   Protein 5g   Fibre 1g   Fat 9g   Sat Fat 4g   Salt 0.1g

300g (10½oz) Greek yogurt
4 tablespoons caster sugar
400g (14oz) seedless red grapes
100ml (3½fl oz) pomegranate
  molasses
50g (1¾oz) pistachio nuts,
  roughly chopped
2 tablespoons clear honey,
  to drizzle

To prepare the labneh, start the day before. Simply line a sieve with a few layers of cheesecloth or muslin. Pour in the Greek yogurt, gather the cloth up and suspend the sieve over a bowl. Excess water will drain from the yogurt overnight giving you a thick, creamy labneh the following day. When ready, stir through 3 tablespoons of the caster sugar.

Preheat the oven to 180°C/350°F/gas mark 4. Place the grapes, pomegranate molasses and remaining 1 tablespoon of sugar into a roasting tin and mix together so that the grapes are evenly coated. Roast for 10–15 minutes, keeping a close eye beyond 10 minutes. You want the grapes to retain their shape and texture, and not collapse too much.

When ready, remove from the oven and cool a little. To serve, spoon the labneh into shallow bowls. Top with the roasted grapes and their juice. Decorate with pistachios and drizzle honey on top to finish.

meringues

Meringues are a thing of beauty — in appearance as well as execution. It is quite fascinating, all that you can achieve with egg whites and sugar.

There are three different types of meringue, differentiated by the way in which they are made and used. The most common one is French meringue. Egg whites are whisked until soft peaks form, caster sugar is added slowly and then whisked until thick and glossy. Italian meringue is made by whisking egg whites until soft peaks form, then slowly pouring in a hot sugar syrup while still whisking, and then the mixture is whisked until cool. This essentially cooks the meringue (the hot sugar syrup cooks the egg whites), so it can be piped straight onto tarts and pies. A blow torch is then often used to crisp up the meringue and give it a beautiful golden colour. Swiss meringue is made by whisking egg whites and sugar together over a saucepan of simmering water, then whisked until cool. I've used French and Italian meringue here.

Beyond the simple marriage of egg white and sugar, the addition of cornflour and/or white wine vinegar, and sometimes cream of tartar, helps to stabilize meringue and give that deliciously chewy interior and crisp shell. This is ultimately personal preference and is not strictly necessary, but in my opinion makes for a better meringue, so I would advise it where the recipe suggests it.

When making meringue, it's important to ensure all of the equipment you are using is scrupulously clean. Any bit of residue on the bowl or whisk you are using will almost surely render your attempt a failure. Although there seems to be a bit of admin prior to getting started with a meringue recipe, this admin is useful knowledge to be armed with in order to achieve success.

There are many recipes out there for meringues which use different quantities of sugar. To reduce the calorie content, I have experimented and have found that 50g (1¾oz) of sugar to one egg white will result in a perfect meringue. A bit more is used when a robust meringue is called for, but as a general rule, this is the ratio used throughout this chapter.

classic meringues

...orks for me every single time and results in meringues
...on the outside and chewy on the inside – my favourite
...en I trained, I learned a novice (albeit messy) way of creating
beautiful meringues using your hands. Scoop up the mixture, enough
for one meringue, and gently clench your fist, with your little finger
toward the tray, to squeeze out the meringue. It creates a very natural,
free-form shape, which I love. To try a differently-textured meringue,
remove from the oven after 50 minutes of cooking. They will have a
very thin outer layer and are beautifully pillowy and soft inside,
like a crunchy cloud.

Makes 12

 calories 74 DF GF V

Carbs 17g Sugar 17g Protein 1g Fibre 0g Fat 0g Sat Fat 0g Salt trace

4 egg whites (approx.
  120g/4¼oz)
small pinch of salt
200g (7oz) caster sugar
¾ tablespoon cornflour
¼ teaspoon white wine vinegar

Preheat the oven to 110°C/225°F/gas mark ¼ and line
a large baking tray with greaseproof paper.

Place the egg whites and salt in the bowl of an electric
stand mixer and whisk on a medium speed until soft
peaks form. Add the sugar, 1 tablespoon at a time, and
when it has all been added, turn the speed to high,
and whisk for about 7–8 minutes, or until the mixture
is smooth when rubbed between your fingers. If it
is grainy, it will need a few minutes longer. Add the
cornflour and vinegar and whisk for a further minute.

Spoon or pipe meringues onto the lined baking tray
and bake for 1½ hours. Turn off the oven and leave the
meringues inside to cool completely. Once cool, peel
off the paper and store in an airtight container until
ready to serve.

iles flottantes (floating islands) with lemon, orange and nutmeg

There is something so delicately sophisticated and elegant about this dessert. It feels almost romantic scooping up luscious spoons of meringue and floating them atop vanilla-specked crème anglaise. After 20 minutes of magic in the oven, the top of each meringue is beautifully crisp, and when broken into, gives way to the most cloud-like meringue you are ever likely to eat.

Serves 8

 calories 176 GF V

Carbs 29g   Sugar 28g   Protein 5g   Fibre 0g   Fat 4g   Sat Fat 2g   Salt 0.2g

400ml (14fl oz) whole milk
200ml (7fl oz) semi-skimmed milk
pared rind of ½ orange
pared rind of ½ lemon
1 vanilla pod, halved and seeds scraped out
½ teaspoon freshly grated nutmeg
3 medium eggs, separated
pinch of salt
200g (7oz) caster sugar
1 teaspoon cornflour

Preheat the oven to 160°C/325°F/gas mark 3. Heat the milks, pared orange and lemon rinds, vanilla pod and seeds and nutmeg in a medium saucepan until just below boiling point.

Meanwhile, to make the meringue, whisk the egg whites in the bowl of an electric stand mixer with a pinch of salt until soft peaks form. Add 180g (6¼oz) of the caster sugar, 1 tablespoon at a time. Whisk for about 8 minutes until the mixture is thick, glossy and totally smooth when rubbed between your fingers.

To make the crème anglaise, in another bowl, whisk the egg yolks, remaining 20g (¾oz) of caster sugar and cornflour together until smooth. Strain the milk and slowly pour onto the egg mixture, whisking all the time. Return to a medium heat and stir until the crème anglaise thickens slightly. It won't be very thick, just enough to lightly coat the back of a spoon.

Pour into a deep oven proof dish, about 30 x 23cm (12 x 9in). Scoop eight nice spoonfuls of the meringue onto the crème anglaise, leaving some space between each one.

Bake for 20 minutes and serve immediately.

blackberry, orange and chocolate meringue mess

You can play around with the types of fruit you use here. Peaches and raspberries would be delicious, as would some cherries. Don't be precious about presentation, it's meant to look messy and indulgent, so have some fun. This could also be served in a big bowl for people to help themselves.

Serves 6

calories 174   GF

Carbs 32g   Sugar 31g   Protein 5g   Fibre 1.5g   Fat 3g   Sat Fat 1.5g   Salt 0.1g

150g (5oz) blackberries
1 tablespoon icing sugar
grated zest of ½ lemon
6 Classic Meringues (see page 92)
40g (1½oz) lemon curd
100g (3½oz) 0% fat Greek yogurt
2 mandarins, peeled
50g (1¾oz) dark chocolate, minimum 70% cocoa solids, melted

Stir together the blackberries, icing sugar and lemon zest and set aside to macerate for 10–15 minutes.

Slice the peeled mandarins into circles, then cut each circle in half to create semicircle shapes.

Prepare six small plates. Lightly crush a meringue on each one. Dot lemon curd and yogurt all over, followed by pieces of mandarin and then the blackberries. Finish with a drizzle of the blackberry juice and melted chocolate. Serve immediately.

chocolate salted caramel swirl meringues

Utterly predictable is my love of salted caramel. No amount of willpower can keep me away if it is within reach — add chocolate and I go weak at the knees.

These meringues are unusual in so far as they are cooked for a very short time. The result is almost marshmallow-like, with a thin crispy exterior and melt-in-your-mouth, light-as-a-feather meringue inside. If you are a fan of chilli, try simmering the caramel with ½ teaspoon of dried chilli flakes, then strain and allow to cool. This piquant layer of flavour is delicious.

Makes 10

 calories 116 GF V

Carbs 23g   Sugar 23g   Protein 2g   Fibre 0g   Fat 2g   Sat Fat 1g   Salt 0.6g

I teaspoon Maldon sea salt
60g (2oz) caramel
20g (¾oz) dark chocolate,
   minimum 80% cocoa solids,
   broken into pieces
4 egg whites (approx. 150g/5oz)
220g (8oz) caster sugar
I teaspoon white wine vinegar

Preheat the oven to 150°C/300°F/gas mark 2. Line two large baking trays with greaseproof paper. Mix ½ teaspoon of the sea salt with the caramel and set aside. Melt the chocolate in a heatproof bowl set over a saucepan of simmering water and set aside to cool.

On a medium speed, whisk the egg whites in the bowl of an electric stand mixer until soft peaks form. Gradually add the sugar, I tablespoon at a time. When added, increase the speed to high and continue whisking for about 8 minutes. Reduce the speed and add the white wine vinegar. Increase the speed again and whisk for another 2 minutes.

Spoon ten meringues onto the trays and drizzle a little of the salted caramel on top. Swirl into the meringue mixture using a knife. Drizzle a little chocolate over each meringue, and again, gently swirl into the meringue. Sprinkle over the remaining sea salt.

Place in the oven and reduce the oven temperature to 120°C/250°F/gas mark ½. Bake for 30 minutes, then turn the oven off and allow to cool for a further 30 minutes in the oven. Set aside to cool.

citrus sesame pavlovas

This recipe is a beautiful balancing act — sour citrus and swe
I have used Greek yogurt here, but if you are not too strict on calor
some whipped cream elevates the recipe even further. This recipe makes
enough for eight, but the pavlovas will keep for a few weeks in an airtight
container, as will the citrus topping, if refrigerated.

Makes 8

 calories 222 GF V

Carbs 49g   Sugar 48g   Protein 5g   Fibre 1g   Fat 0g   Sat Fat 0g   Salt 0.2g

pinch of salt
4 egg whites (approx. 150g/5oz)
200g (7oz) caster sugar
¾ tablespoon cornflour
¼ teaspoon white wine vinegar
grated zest of 1 lemon
1 teaspoon black sesame seeds
100g (3½oz) 0% fat Greek
  yogurt

For the citrus topping
1 lemon
1 lime
1 orange (blood orange if in
  season)
50g (1¾oz) sugar
100ml (3½fl oz) water
3 mandarins
2 pink grapefruit

Note: For a more traditional
pavlova, serve with cream
and strawberries and some
very thinly pared strips of
lemon rind.

Preheat the oven to 140°C/275°F/gas mark 1. Line a
large baking tray with greaseproof paper and set aside.

To the bowl of an electric stand mixer, add the salt
and egg whites. Whisk until soft peaks form and then
add the sugar, 1 tablespoon at a time. When it has all
been added, increase the speed and whisk for about 8
minutes, or until the mixture is totally smooth when
rubbed between your fingers (if it is still grainy it needs
longer.) Add the cornflour and vinegar and whisk for
a further minute. Very gently fold in the lemon zest
and spoon eight dollops onto the baking tray. Spread
out with the back of a spoon, leaving enough space to
expand in the oven. Sprinkle over the sesame seeds.

Place in the middle of the oven and cook for 2 hours.
When ready, turn off the oven and leave to cool inside.

Meanwhile, make the topping. Peel the skin and pith
from the lemon, lime and orange. Cut the flesh into
thin slices, removing any seeds as you go. Place in a
saucepan with the sugar and water, bring to the boil and
simmer very gently for about 5 minutes, or until the
sugar is dissolved (no more than 10 minutes). Peel and
slice the mandarins as above. Segment the grapefruit.
Add to the syrup mixture, stir and cool completely.

To serve, place a generous spoonful of yogurt onto each
pavlova, followed by the citrus topping and the juice.
Serve immediately.

layered mocha meringue cake

This cake is designed for a crowd – great to look at, even better to eat and, most of all, pretty simple to make. You will in no way feel that this is a low-calorie dessert. It tastes as indulgent as it looks.

Serves 12

 calories 218 GF V

Carbs 40g   Sugar 37g   Protein 5g   Fibre 0g   Fat 5g   Sat Fat 3g   Salt 0.1g

10 medium egg whites
400g (14oz) caster sugar
1 tablespoon cornflour
1 tablespoon white wine vinegar
250g (9oz) plain fromage frais
30ml (1fl oz) chicory and
   coffee essence (such as
   Camp)
100ml (3½fl oz) whipping
   cream
30g (1oz) dark chocolate,
   minimum 70% cocoa solids,
   broken into pieces
10g (½oz) cocoa powder

Line two 30 x 20cm (12 x 8in) Swiss roll tins with greaseproof paper. Preheat the oven to 160°C/325°F/gas mark 3. Place the egg whites in the bowl of an electric stand mixer. Whisk until soft peaks form. Gradually add the sugar, 1 tablespoon at a time. Once added, whisk the mixture on the highest speed for 7–8 minutes, or until the mixture is silky smooth when rubbed between your index finger and thumb (if you can feel any grains of sugar, you need to whisk a little longer). Mix the cornflour and vinegar together and add to the mixture. Whisk for a further minute and then divide the meringue between the two prepared tins, spreading it out with a spatula or palette knife. Bake for 25 minutes, and then allow to cool completely in the tin.

When ready to assemble the cake, mix the fromage frais with the chicory coffee essence. Lightly whip the cream until soft peaks form and gently fold in the fromage frais mixture. Melt the chocolate in a heatproof bowl set over a saucepan of simmering water.

Slice each sheet of meringue in half lengthways. Place one piece onto a platter. Spoon one third of the coffee cream on top and spread out. Repeat with each layer except for the top. Dust the final layer of meringue with cocoa and then drizzle the melted chocolate all over. Allow the chocolate to cool and harden before serving. This cake is best eaten on the day it is made.

lime almond meringues

The addition of brown sugar to these meringues gives them a very subtle caramel flavour, which is lovely with the almonds. If you want to dress these up a little, serve with slices of fresh, ripe mango and a spoonful of yogurt or whipped cream.

Makes 18

 calories 103 DF GF V

Carbs 15g   Sugar 14g   Protein 3.5g   Fibre 0g   Fat 4g   Sat Fat 0.5g   Salt trace

120g (4¼oz) flaked almonds
125g (4½oz) caster sugar
75g (2½oz) soft light brown sugar
50g (1¾oz) icing sugar
4 medium egg whites
small pinch of salt
1 tablespoon cornflour
grated zest of 2 limes

Preheat the oven to 110°C/225°F/gas mark ½. Line two baking trays with greaseproof paper. Toast the almonds in a dry frying pan until golden brown. Transfer to a baking tray or plate and allow to cool completely.

In a food-processor, blitz the three sugars together until fine. This step is important to remove any lumps from the brown sugar and to ensure they are all uniform when added to the egg whites.

In the bowl of an electric stand mixer, whisk the egg whites with a small pinch of salt until soft peaks form. Add the sugar, 1 tablespoon at a time, and whisk on a high speed for about 8 minutes. Add the cornflour and whisk for another minute.

Mix the lime zest with the almonds, ensuring it is evenly dispersed. Gently fold three-quarters of them into the meringue mixture.

Spoon 18 meringues in total onto the lined baking trays. Use the back of a small spoon to flatten each one slightly. Scatter with the remaining almonds and bake for 1½ hours. Leave to cool in the oven.

mango, lime and coconut baked alaskas

This is all about the mango, so try to find beautiful ripe ones to get the best flavour. This sorbet doesn't melt anywhere near as fast as traditional ice cream, so you have time to pipe your meringue once it is out of the freezer. There is so little sponge used that it doesn't make sense to bake it especially.

Serves 4

calories 272

V

Carbs 57g   Sugar 50g   Protein 2.5g   Fibre 2g   Fat 3.5g   Sat Fat 2g   Salt 0.2g

1 shop-bought Madeira cake
1 large ripe mango (approx.
    200g/7oz), peeled, stoned,
    cut into wedges and frozen
3 tablespoons maple syrup
grated zest and juice of 1 lime
dried coconut flakes, to
    decorate (optional)

For the Italian meringue
220g (8oz) caster sugar
¼ teaspoon cream of tartar
2 egg whites

Note: The Italian meringue makes more than you need, but it is easier and more reliable to make in this larger quantity. To make a quirky treat, place a chocolate liqueur onto a cocktail stick, dip in the Italian meringue and blow torch until golden. This makes for a delicious petit four.

Cut two 6cm (2½in) round circles from the Madeira cake and then slice so that each one is 1cm (½in) thick.

Remove the mango from the freezer and allow to soften for about 10 minutes. Transfer to a food-processor and blitz with the maple syrup and lime zest and juice, until the consistency is like sorbet. If it is not happening, simply let the mango defrost a little more, but not totally. It is important for it to remain mostly frozen to get the right consistency and to be able to scoop it. Scoop into six balls, slightly bigger than a golf ball, place on a lined tray and return to the freezer.

When ready to serve, make the meringue. Put the sugar and cream of tartar with 40ml (1½fl oz) water in a small saucepan over a medium heat. Swirl gently every now and then to encourage the sugar to dissolve. Place a sugar thermometer in the pan and boil until the temperature reaches 122°C/252°F.

Whisk the egg whites in the bowl of an electric stand mixer until soft peaks form, then add the sugar syrup in a slow steady stream, continuously whisking on a high speed until the mixture has cooled and is thick and glossy. Transfer to a piping bag fitted with a small round nozzle.

Place a scoop of sorbet onto each sponge circle. Pipe the meringue all around and over each one to cover. Using a blow torch, scorch the meringue all over, so that it is golden brown. Garnish with coconut flakes, if using, and serve immediately.

lemon thyme meringue cake

This cake is baked in two stages and has two layers — a dense but delicately fragrant lemon thyme base piled high with beautiful pillowy meringue that has a fantastic crispy top when baked. Despite consisting of a few steps, it is very easy to make. And very difficult to stop at one slice! To make this cake gluten-free, use all ground almonds and a gluten-free baking powder.

Serves 10

calories
298

V

Carbs 40g   Sugar 34g   Protein 7g   Fibre 0g   Fat 12g   Sat Fat 5g   Salt 0.3g

80g (3oz) unsalted butter, plus
  extra for greasing
120g (4½oz) caster sugar
grated zest of 2 lemons
1 vanilla pod, halved and seeds
  scraped out
4–5 sprigs of lemon thyme,
  leaves picked
3 medium eggs, separated
60g (2oz) ground almonds
60g (2oz) self-raising flour
½ teaspoon baking powder
200g (7oz) natural yogurt
pinch of salt
fresh raspberries and toasted
  flaked almonds, to decorate
  (optional)

For the meringue topping
4 egg whites
pinch of salt
200g (7oz) caster sugar
1 teaspoon white wine vinegar
1 tablespoon cornflour

Preheat the oven to 160°C/325°F/gas mark 3. Line the base of a 24cm (9½in) spring-form tin and grease the sides with some butter.

Put half the sugar with the butter, lemon zest, vanilla seeds and thyme leaves in an electric stand mixer. Whisk until pale and creamy. Scrape down the sides of the bowl before adding the egg yolks, one at a time, whisking for a few minutes as you add them. Add the ground almonds, flour and baking powder and whisk to combine. Gently fold in the natural yogurt.

In a separate bowl, whisk the egg whites with a pinch of salt until soft peaks form. Add the remaining sugar, 1 tablespoon at a time, and whisk until thick and glossy. Gently fold a few spoonfuls into the cake mixture and follow with the remaining mixture. Pour into the prepared cake tin and bake for 30 minutes.

Start making the meringue topping 5 minutes before the cake is ready. Whisk the egg whites with a pinch of salt until soft peaks form, then add the sugar, 1 tablespoon at a time until all incorporated. Continue whisking the mixture until thick, glossy and smooth. Add the vinegar and cornflour and whisk for a few seconds more. Spoon over the cake and bake for a further 25 minutes.

Allow the cake to cool completely in the tin before serving. Top with raspberries and almonds, if you wish.

mystery torte

This recipe was given to me by my mother-in-law, Lizzie. I love the name
of it; if it was simply served to you, you would do very well to detect the
ingredients. The salty Ritz crackers provide a delicious counterbalance to
the sweet meringue — a genius stroke. Furthermore, anything filled with
walnuts is a winner in my book. This is an unusual one and not really like
a cake or torte. It is not even much like meringue. I guess you will
just have to make it to see what it is really like!

Serves 8

 calories 286

Carbs 34g   Sugar 27g   Protein 4.5g   Fibre 1.5g   Fat 14.5g   Sat Fat 6g   Salt 0.3g

12 Ritz crackers
60g (2oz) walnuts
4 egg whites
pinch of salt
200g (7oz) caster sugar
1 teaspoon baking powder

To serve
150ml (5fl oz) whipping cream,
   whipped until soft peaks
   form
150g (5oz) mixed berries, such
   as raspberries, strawberries
   and blueberries

Preheat the oven to 180°C/350°F/gas mark 4.
Grease and line a 20cm (8in) round spring-form tin.

Roughly chop the crackers and walnuts, or pulse for
a short time in a small food-processor.

Whisk the egg whites with a pinch of salt until soft peaks
form. Add the sugar, 1 tablespoon at a time, until all of
it is incorporated and then whisk for about 7 minutes.
The mixture should feel smooth when rubbed between
your fingers. If not, continue whisking for a few
minutes more. Add the baking powder and whisk
for a further minute.

Working as gently as possible so as to not knock
out any air from the meringue, fold in the chopped
crackers and nuts. Pour into the prepared tin,
flatten the surface and bake for 50 minutes.

Top with the cream and berries and serve.

berry and saffron honey roulade

A roulade is one of my go-to recipes; easy to throw together, looks good and always delivers on taste. The saffron honey is an extra, but a very worthwhile one. The delicate flavour of saffron with berries is surprisingly delicious.

Serves 8

 calories 220

Carbs 34g Sugar 34g Protein 5g Fibre 1g Fat 7g Sat Fat 2.5g Salt 0.1g

40g (1½oz) hazelnuts
60g (2oz) clear honey
large pinch of saffron threads
10g (½oz) icing sugar
100g (3½oz) raspberries
70g (2½oz) blueberries
4 egg whites (approx. 150g/5oz)
pinch of salt
200g (7oz) caster sugar
seeds of ½ vanilla pod
150ml (5fl oz) 0% fat Greek
   yogurt
70ml (3fl oz) whipping cream,
   whipped to soft peaks

Preheat the oven to 200°C/400°F/gas mark 6. Line a 30 x 20cm (12 x 8in) Swiss roll tin with greaseproof paper. Place the hazelnuts on a baking tray and roast for about 5 minutes. Rub between a tea towel to remove the skins. Don't worry about removing them all; it looks pretty with some of the skins left on. Roughly chop.

Place the honey and saffron in a small saucepan and place over a medium heat. When the honey is bubbling, turn off the heat and set aside to infuse. In a medium bowl, stir the icing sugar into the berries and set aside to macerate.

In the bowl of an electric stand mixer, whisk the egg whites and salt until soft peaks form. Add the sugar, 1 tablespoon at a time. Increase the speed to high and whisk for about 8 minutes, or until smooth. If it is still grainy, it needs a little longer. Scoop into the tin and spread out evenly. Bake for 25 minutes until crisp and slightly golden. Leave to cool in the tin for 5 minutes.

Very carefully turn upside down onto a large sheet of greaseproof paper. Allow to cool for 10–15 minutes. Meanwhile, tip the fruit into a sieve set over a bowl to strain off the juice. Stir the vanilla seeds into the yogurt, then fold in the whipped cream. When the roulade is cool, spread over the cream mixture and the berries. Using the greaseproof paper to help you, roll into a log, working from the longest edge. Chill for 30 minutes.

To serve, transfer to a serving plate. Gently warm the honey and drizzle all over the roulade. Sprinkle the hazelnuts on top and serve immediately with a spoonful of the berry juices. This is best eaten on the same day.

pear and pistachio meringue sandwiches

These little meringue sandwiches are a gorgeous way to enjoy a very simple but utterly satisfying treat. Pistachio nibs are vibrantly green and come thinly sliced. You can also use shelled pistachio nuts instead.

Makes 6

Carbs 36g   Sugar 36g   Protein 6.5g   Fibre 1g   Fat 6.5g   Sat Fat 2g   Salt 0.1g

3 large egg whites (approx. 125g/4½oz)
pinch of salt
¼ teaspoon cream of tartar
150g (5oz) golden caster sugar
50g (1¾oz) white chocolate, melted to decorate
50g (1¾oz) pistachio nibs (or pistachio nuts), blitzed to a crumb
seeds of 1 vanilla pod
100g (3½oz) 0% fat Greek yogurt
2 ripe pears
squeeze of lemon juice

Preheat the oven to 120°C/250°F/gas mark ½.

Cut out two pieces of greaseproof paper to line two large baking trays. Draw in pencil 12 9cm (3½in) diameter circles on one side and place the drawn side face down onto the tray, ensuring you can see the circles from the other side.

Whisk the egg whites, salt and cream of tartar in an electric stand mixer until soft peaks form. On a medium speed, add the sugar, 1 tablespoon at a time. Increase the speed to high and whisk for about 8 minutes. The meringue is ready when the mixture rubbed between your fingers is totally smooth and not at all grainy.

Spoon into a piping bag fitted with a wide round nozzle and pipe into the circles on the greaseproof paper. Smooth over with the back of a spoon. (Alternatively, just spoon the mixture into the circles and spread out with a spatula.) Bake for 1½ hours. Allow the meringues to cool in the oven.

When ready to serve, dip the edge of each meringue in the melted white chocolate and then roll in the pistachio crumb.

Stir the vanilla seeds into the yogurt. Core and slice the pears thinly and dress with a little lemon juice to stop them from browning. Spoon some yogurt onto the inside of a meringue, add a few slices of pear and top with another meringue. Repeat. Serve immediately.

toffee peach pavlova

The muscovado sugar creates a decadent toffee-like flavour throughout this pavlova. Use the very best, ripe peaches you can find. When blended, they create the most beautifully silky smooth purée. A little cream goes a long way here, as no pavlova is truly complete without.

Serves 12

calories 145 GF V

Carbs 22g   Sugar 22g   Protein 3g   Fibre 2g   Fat 4.5g   Sat Fat 3g   Salt 0.1g

115g (4oz) caster sugar
85g (3oz) dark muscovado sugar
4 egg whites
pinch of salt
8 ripe peaches
100g (3½fl oz) double cream
70g (2½oz) 0% fat Greek yogurt
100g (3½oz) raspberries
fresh mint leaves, to serve

Preheat the oven to 160°C/325°F/gas mark 3. On a piece of greaseproof paper the same size as your baking tray, draw a circle in pencil about 23cm (9in) across. Place the drawn side face down, ensuring the circle is visible.

Place the sugars together in a small blender and blitz. This breaks up the larger chunks of the muscovado, ensuring it mixes evenly. Whisk the egg whites and salt in the bowl of an electric stand mixer until soft peaks form. On a medium speed, whisk in the sugar, 1 tablespoon at time. Increase the speed to high and whisk for about 8 minutes. Rub a little mixture between your fingers – it should be totally smooth, not at all grainy.

Spread the mixture onto the lined baking tray, filling the circle. Place in the oven, immediately reduce the temperature to 120°C/250°F/gas mark ½ and bake for 2½ hours. Turn off the oven and allow to cool completely before you take it out.

Using a sharp knife, cut a cross into the base of half the peaches. Cover with boiling water and simmer for 5 minutes. Drain, cool, and peel. Discard the stones and blitz the flesh in a blender until silky smooth.

Just before serving, whip the cream until soft peaks form, then fold in the yogurt. Stone and thinly slice the remaining peaches. Place the pavlova onto a serving plate, spoon over the cream, then the peach purée, and top with the sliced peaches, raspberries and mint leaves.

frozen

Ice cream is a dessert you can always have a bit of fun with, and there isn't a whole lot that can go wrong.

These desserts come in all shapes and sizes. From a frozen ice cream pie taking inspiration from the flavours of a black forest gateaux, to a very simple and elegant semifreddo flavoured with little more than caramelized honey. Get your hands on a few ice pop moulds for the Malt Milkshake Pops and the Lemon Buttermilk Sherbet Pops; these two are great in summer months and tick the box for adults and children alike.

Frozen yogurt is so easy to make and, when made properly, is utterly delicious and a great substitute to a heavier, custard-based ice cream. The trick is to get ahead and strain the yogurt a day in advance. This removes excess water from the yogurt and gives a creamier more ice cream-like froyo. Transfer to ice pop moulds and then cover in chocolate before serving to make sophisticated Chocolate Vanilla Froyo Pops, or swirl delicious cherry syrup through to achieve a decadent Cherry Ripple Frozen Yogurt.

A little trick with fruit is to pop it in the freezer and then blitz it to make a really delicious type of sorbet. It is very simple and works really well with berries, kiwifruit, bananas and mangoes. Very low calorie and when dressed up into something special, as with the Frozen Kiwi, Melon and Mint Ice Bar, it makes for an impressive and satisfying dessert.

I would advise getting yourself an ice-cream maker. There are loads that are not at all expensive and make the process of ice cream making very simple indeed.

black forest ice cream pie

This ice cream pie uses the Cherry Ripple Frozen Yogurt from page 117.
However, if you want to cheat, you can buy some vanilla frozen yogurt,
make the cherry syrup as per this recipe and combine the two.
Mix them together in a blender when the yogurt is frozen and
you should then have a spreadable mixture.

Serves 10

 calories 270 V

Carbs 40g   Sugar 31g   Protein 7g   Fibre 1g   Fat 9g   Sat Fat 5g   Salt 0.2g

200g (7oz) Bourbon cream
biscuits
500g (18oz) vanilla frozen
yogurt
½ quantity Cherry Ripple
Frozen Yogurt (page 117)
60g (2oz) dark chocolate,
minimum 70% cocoa solids,
broken into pieces
1 tablespoon kirsch
100g (3½oz) fresh cherries,
mixed varieties if possible
20g (¾oz) mixed white and
dark chocolate, finely grated
to serve (optional)

Blitz the Bourbon cream biscuits in a blender until you
have fine crumbs. Add 40ml (1½fl oz) water and pulse
once or twice. Spread all over the base of a 20cm (8in)
fluted loose-based tin, pressing it in tightly with the
back of a spoon, and then refrigerate to set.

Remove the vanilla frozen yogurt from the freezer
and sit at room temperature to soften slightly before
blitzing in a food-processor to a consistency that allows
you to spread it easily. Spread all over the biscuit base
and freeze until set.

Repeat the same step with the cherry ripple frozen
yogurt. Freeze again.

When ready to serve, make the chocolate syrup.
Melt the chocolate in a heatproof bowl set over a
saucepan of simmering water, ensuring the bowl
does not tough the water. Stir in the kirsch.

Remove the ice cream cake from the freezer and place
on a serving dish. Pour the chocolate syrup all over.
Top with fresh cherries and finish with grated white
and dark chocolate, if you like.

caramelized honey semifreddo with nectarines

This is almost like a cheat's honeycomb type of ice cream. Caramelizing the honey makes it sticky and almost ready to set. When you pour it into the whipped cream mixture and freeze it, it marbles beautifully through the semifreddo and is crunchy when eaten. The flavours here are simple, as is the process. It's not quite a classic version of a semifreddo as I have left out egg yolks, but it works without, and takes down the calorie content significantly.

Serves 10

 calories 196 GF V

Carbs 21g   Sugar 21g   Protein 2.5g   Fibre 0.4g   Fat 11g   Sat Fat 7g   Salt trace

150g (5oz) clear honey
280ml (9½fl oz) whipping cream
1 tablespoon vanilla bean paste
4 medium egg whites (approx. 120g/4½oz)
70g (2½oz) caster sugar
2–3 ripe nectarines, stoned and cut into wedges

Line a 450g (1lb) loaf tin with a few layers of clingfilm, ensuring there are no gaps and that there is enough left hanging over the sides to encase the semifreddo.

Place the honey in a small, heavy-based saucepan and boil until it turns a deep bronze colour. Be careful to not let it burn. Remove from the heat and allow to cool slightly while you prepare the other ingredients.

In one bowl, whip the cream with the vanilla bean paste until soft peaks form. In another, whisk the egg whites until soft peaks form. Then add the sugar in a slow, steady stream and continue whisking for 3–4 minutes, until thick and glossy.

Fold the egg white mixture into the cream mixture. Then drizzle the caramelized honey all over. Don't mix it in. Simply pour the mixture into the prepared tin. The honey will marble into the cream as you pour.

Cover with clingfilm and freeze until firm. Remove from the freezer about 20 minutes before you are ready to serve. Slice and serve with the nectarines.

cherry ripple frozen yogurt

The purpose of straining the yogurt here is to remove as much liquid from it as possible, making it freeze better when it is churned. If cherries are in season, by all means use them. Some fresh cherries stirred through at the end would be nice, too. A few tablespoons of kirsch will up the ante on the cherry flavour if you have any lying around in your cupboard.

Serves 8

calories 178 GF V

Carbs 25g   Sugar 25g   Protein 8g   Fibre 0.5g   Fat 5g   Sat Fat 3.5g   Salt 0.1g

400g (14oz) full-fat Greek yogurt
350g (12oz) 0% fat Greek yogurt
350g (12oz) frozen cherries
100g (3½oz) caster sugar
30g (1oz) soft light brown sugar
1 teaspoon vanilla bean paste

The day before you are ready to make this frozen yogurt, line a sieve with a few layers of cheesecloth or muslin and pour in the yogurts. Gather the edges of the cloth up and fold over the top. Suspend the sieve over a bowl and leave in the fridge overnight.

Place the cherries, sugars and vanilla bean paste in a medium saucepan and place over a medium heat. Stir to mix and slowly bring to the boil. Simmer for about 10 minutes, then remove from the heat and allow to cool completely. When ready, blitz until smooth and then pass through a sieve, pressing through as much of the liquid as possible.

Set aside 75g (2¾oz) of the cherry syrup. Remove the yogurt from the cheesecloth and stir into the remaining quantity of syrup using a whisk to help incorporate everything. Churn in your ice-cream maker according to the manufacturer's instructions, and when ready, transfer to a tub that is suitable for freezing. Ripple through the reserved cherry syrup, cover with a tight-fitting lid and then freeze until firm. Allow to sit for 20 minutes at room temperature before you serve it in scoops.

chocolate vanilla froyo pops

My favourite way to have frozen yogurt is fresh from the ice-cream maker, softly served, or made into these refreshing pops, covered with chocolate. It is very easy to make, but to get the best results you need to be organized and start a day ahead to strain the yogurt. I have used a combination of full-fat and 0 per cent fat Greek yogurt here.

Makes 8

 calories 209 GF V

Carbs 22g   Sugar 22g   Protein 10g   Fibre 0g   Fat 9g   Sat Fat 6g   Salt 0.2g

500g (18oz) full-fat Greek yogurt
500g (18oz) 0% fat Greek yogurt
90g (3½oz) caster sugar
seeds from 1 vanilla pod
70g (2½oz) dark chocolate, minimum 70% cocoa solids, melted

The day before you plan to make these, you need to strain the yogurt. Line a sieve with a few layers of cheesecloth or muslin. Pour the yogurts into the lined sieve, gather the cloth up and fold over the top. Suspend the sieve over a bowl and leave in the fridge overnight.

The following day, discard the liquid in the bowl and transfer the thick yogurt to a clean bowl. Stir in the sugar and vanilla seeds. Transfer to an ice-cream maker and churn until almost set – to the point where it is like soft-serve ice cream.

Spoon into ice-cream moulds and freeze until firm.

When frozen, remove from the moulds, place on a lined baking tray and drizzle the melted chocolate all over. Refreeze until ready to serve.

celebrating strawberries with sorbet

This cool refreshing sorbet served with the best strawberries the season has to offer is a true homage to this wonderful fruit. Strawberries can be found in supermarkets almost all year round now, but this kind of forced production simply does not produce anything like the fruit that nature's seasons give us. Seasonal berries are crucial to the success of this recipe.

Serves 6

calories 129   DF   GF   V   VE

Carbs 26g   Sugar 26g   Protein 1g   Fibre 6g   Fat 0g   Sat Fat 0g   Salt 0g

100g (3½oz) caster sugar
1kg (2lb 4oz) strawberries
juice of ½ lemon

Place the sugar in a small saucepan with 30ml (1fl oz) water and place over a medium heat. Stir to encourage the sugar to dissolve into a clear syrup. When ready, set aside to cool.

Wash, dry and hull 750g (1lb 10oz) of the strawberries. Using a handheld blender, blitz until completely smooth. Pass through a fine sieve using the back of a soup ladle to press as much of the juice and purée through as possible.

Stir in the sugar syrup and lemon juice and chill. Churn in an ice-cream maker until set and then pour into a freezerproof container and freeze. Remove from the freezer about 15 minutes before you are ready to serve with the remaining sliced strawberries.

fruit sorbets

Most fruits can be frozen and then blitzed to create delicious ice creams, which in truth are more like a sorbet. Either way, they are delicious, simple to throw together, healthy and low calorie.

blackberry and orange

Serves 8 calories 59

Carbs 12g   Sugar 11g   Protein 0.7g   Fibre 3g   Fat 0g   Sat Fat 0g   Salt 0g

600g (1lb 5oz) frozen blackberries
5 tablespoons maple syrup
grated zest of 2 oranges and juice of ½
½ tablespoon vanilla bean paste

Place the frozen blackberries, maple syrup, orange zest and juice and vanilla bean paste into a food-processor and pulse until silky smooth. Transfer to a freezerproof container and freeze until needed. Remove from the freezer 10 minutes before you are ready to serve to soften slightly.

banana, coconut and passion fruit

Serves 6

 calories 64 DF GF V VE

. . . .

Carbs 10g   Sugar 8.8g   Protein 0.6g   Fibre 0.9g   Fat 0.4g   Sat Fat 0.3g   Salt trace

. . . .

4 medium ripe bananas, sliced
40ml (1½fl oz) reduced-fat
   coconut milk
seeds of 2 passion fruits

Freeze the slices of banana until firm.

When ready, allow to sit at room temperature for about 5 minutes before blitzing in a food-processor with the coconut milk, until smooth and thick. Stir in the passion fruit seeds, transfer to a freezerproof tub and freeze until needed.

kiwi, melon and mint

Serves 8

 calories 86 DF GF V VE

. . . .

Carbs 19g   Sugar 19g   Protein 0.7g   Fibre 1.5g   Fat 0g   Sat Fat 0g   Salt 0g

. . . .

6 kiwifruit, peeled and cut into
   chunks
½ galia melon (approx.
   350g/12oz), peeled,
   deseeded and cut into chunks
100g (3½oz) caster sugar
4 sprigs of mint, leaves picked

Place all the fruit in a freezer bag and freeze until firm. When ready, bring the sugar and 100ml (3½fl oz) water to the boil in a saucepan and simmer until the sugar has dissolved. Cool until it is just lukewarm (a quick way to do this is to place the saucepan in a basin of cold water).

While the sugar syrup is cooling, remove the fruit from the freezer to soften a little. Place in a food-processor along with the mint leaves and blitz, pouring in the sugar syrup slowly. Continue blending until completely cooled.

It should have a soft serve texture, meaning you could have it straight away, or you could give it a few more hours in a freezerproof tub in the freezer to firm up before serving.

chocolate rosemary gelato pots with pear crisps

While I was training, I made a rosemary pannacotta with chocolate wafers and fresh pears. It's still one of my favourite flavour combinations, reimagined here.

Serves 10

 calories 171 GF V

Carbs 19g   Sugar 19g   Protein 4.5g   Fibre 0g   Fat 8g   Sat Fat 4g   Salt trace

750ml (25fl oz) whole milk
3 sprigs of rosemary
100g (3½oz) dark chocolate,
    minimum 70% cocoa solids,
    broken into pieces
5 medium egg yolks
100g (3½oz) caster sugar

For the pear crisps
2 pears
juice of 1 lemon mixed with
    3 tablespoons cold water
1 tablespoon caster sugar

Note: dip the pear crisps in melted chocolate, allow to set, and serve as a super low calorie petit four.

In a medium saucepan, slowly bring the milk and rosemary to just below boiling point. Turn the heat right down and infuse for 10 minutes, then strain.

Melt the chocolate in a heatproof bowl set over a saucepan of simmering water, ensuring it does not touch the water. Remove from the heat, slowly whisk in the milk, then return to the pan and keep warm.

Whisk the egg yolks with the sugar until thick and creamy. Slowly stir in the warm chocolate milk, return to the saucepan and place over a medium heat. Stir until thick enough to coat the back of a spoon, up to 5 minutes. Do not boil, or it will curdle. Cool completely, then place in an ice-cream maker and churn until softly set. The time this takes will depend on your machine. Pour into a tub and freeze until set.

Meanwhile, make the pear crisps. Preheat the oven to 110°C/225°F/gas mark ¼. Line two baking trays with greaseproof paper. Using a mandoline, slice the pears lengthways about 5mm (¼in) thick, adding them to the lemon water as you go. Leave for 10 minutes, then drain and pat dry on clean tea towels. Lay flat on the prepared baking trays, sprinkle with sugar and bake for 1 hour. Keep a close eye as oven temperatures will vary. They will curl up around the edges and be light golden brown when ready. Leave to cool and crisp up on the baking trays, then store in an airtight container. Serve the gelato alongside three pear crisps per serving.

malt milkshake pops

Malt milkshakes were a late discovery for me. I have no idea how, but once I tried them, I fell hard. These are as good for grown-ups as they are for kids, and there will be a fight to get to the front of the queue.

Serves 6

Carbs 21g   Sugar 11.5g   Protein 4g   Fibre 0g   Fat 10g   Sat Fat 5g   Salt 0.4g

370ml (13fl oz) unsweetened almond milk
150ml (5fl oz) single cream
25g (1oz) icing sugar
75g (2½oz) Horlicks light
40g (1½oz) chocolate, melted
40g (1½oz) Maltesers, crushed

In a saucepan, gently heat the almond milk and cream. Whisk the icing sugar and Horlicks powder into the hot liquid. Allow to cool, and then transfer to moulds.

When ready to serve, remove from the moulds and dip the top of each pop into the melted chocolate, followed by the crushed Maltesers. Leave to set, then serve.

lemon buttermilk sherbet pops

These perfectly capture the refreshing qualities of buttermilk and lemon. The praline adds sweetness and crunch, but is optional.

Serves 4

Carbs 30g   Sugar 30g   Protein 4g   Fibre 0g   Fat 2.5g   Sat Fat 0.5g   Salt 0.1g

130g (4½oz) clear honey
zest of 1 lemon and juice of 2
1 sprig of rosemary
385ml (13½fl oz) buttermilk
40g (1½oz) Pistachio, Almond and Rosemary Praline (see page 148), crushed (optional)

Note: shop bought praline could also be used here.

Place the honey, lemon zest and juice and rosemary in a saucepan and boil. Remove from the heat and cool slightly, then add the buttermilk. Strain and cool completely. Churn in an ice-cream maker according to the manufacturer's instructions. When it is thick like a slush puppy, pour into ice-pop moulds and freeze.

Remove from the freezer, and allow to soften slightly if dipping in praline. Remove from the moulds. Dip the ice pops into the praline just before serving.

frozen kiwi, melon and mint ice bar

I like to serve these in summertime when we are in the garden and craving something fresh and simple. Of course, you can use any of the fruit sorbets here. Equally, use whatever nuts you prefer in the base. This is definitely one that is open to interpretation.

Serves 10

Carbs 22g   Sugar 22g   Protein 4g   Fibre 2g   Fat 8g   Sat Fat 3g   Salt trace

50g (1¾oz) blanched almonds
50g (1¾oz) pistachios
45g (1½oz) dried coconut flakes
4 medium dates, stoned
1 tablespoon clear honey
1 quantity Kiwi, Melon and Mint Fruit Sorbet (page 123)
100g (3½oz) vanilla frozen yogurt (page 118 or use shop-bought)

Line an 18cm (7in) square, 2.5cm (1in) deep loose-based tin with greaseproof paper.

Place the nuts, coconut flakes, dates and honey in a food-processor and blitz until you have a chunky paste. Add a little hot water if necessary. Scoop the nut mixture into the prepared tin and press over the base and into all the corners, making it as flat and even as possible.

Remove the kiwi, melon and mint sorbet from the freezer and allow it to soften enough for you to scoop and spread it. Spread it all over the nut base and freeze until firm.

When frozen, cover with the slightly softened vanilla frozen yogurt. Freeze until firm.

When ready, remove from the tin, cut into ten slices and serve.

coffee granita with cream and kumquats

I like to use really strong coffee for this recipe so the granita tastes more like a strong, slightly sweetened granita, rather than an overly sweet one, with only a hint of coffee flavour. Kumquats make for a delicious accompaniment. I like the outer skin, but they have to be sliced wafer thin for it to work. Use a really sharp knife for this. If you can't find kumquats, use some finely chopped orange instead.

Serves 6

 calories 114 GF V

Carbs 12g   Sugar 12g   Protein 0.5g   Fibre 0.8g   Fat 7g   Sat Fat 4g   Salt trace

550ml (19fl oz) freshly brewed espresso coffee
60g (2oz) caster sugar
100ml (3½ fl oz) whipping cream, whipped until soft peaks form
6–7 kumquats, thinly sliced

Note: this is not the sweetest of desserts. It is, in essence, another way of serving a strong coffee. However, if you want to make it sweeter, add 1 tablespoon of icing sugar to the cream prior to whipping.

If the coffee you have just brewed is still really hot, stir in the sugar and it will dissolve. If not, place in a saucepan to heat and then stir in the sugar. Transfer to a freezerproof container, and allow to cool. Then place in the freezer for 3–4 hours, or until it is almost, but not completely, frozen.

Transfer to a food-processor and blitz until you have fine crystals of ice. Return to the freezer and freeze until firm.

Just before you are ready to serve, allow the granita to sit at room temperature for about 10 minutes. Scrape the surface with a fork and spoon the granita into bowls (it helps to chill the bowls prior to serving to stop the granita from melting too quickly). Serve each portion with a spoonful of cream and some kumquats slices.

petit fours and small bites

Some meals require nothing more than a touch of sweetness, something small and delicate, to wrap everything up. Petit fours are a great way of serving something sweet. Most are prepared in advance and they encourage a kind of informal sharing. I generally serve mine with a strong coffee, or tea, depending on guest's preferences, and sit back and enjoy the relaxation that comes over everyone after a great meal. What could be better than coffee, something sweet, and wonderful conversation?

Chocolate truffles two ways: one with sour cherries and freeze-dried raspberries, the other with salted miso. The latter should be served with caution, and with enough to satisfy greedy hands. The combination of dark chocolate, miso, salt and golden syrup is highly addictive! A touch of class can be offered in the form of Lemon and Lavender Macarons. Fear not — there are far more challenging things than achieving the perfect macaron (even if they are a little less than perfect, they still taste great.) Very simple Sesame, Ginger and Vanilla Biscuits are a palate-cleansing light bite, and if you are really craving a hit of sugar, chilli popcorn honeycomb is what you need.

This chapter is also dedicated to certain treats which are personal favourites of mine, which are not necessarily petit fours, but appear here as 'small bites'. In truth, they are not actually that small. Sugar-coated doughnuts (deep-fried, the traditional, and only way in my mind) and Lemon and Juniper Portuguese Custard Tarts are ever so slightly smaller than you might find them elsewhere, but lacking none of the indulgence. Chocolate Cannoli are a real touch of indulgence and won't want to be shared! All three feel and taste anything but low calorie, so if you want to show off a bit, these are just the ticket!

chocolate cannoli

I first had these at a food market local to me. They are a Sicilian trademark, the pastry traditionally made with lard and marsala, and filled with a sweetened ricotta. These vary slightly from the traditional ones, but are still delicious.

Makes 12

 calories 160

 V

Carbs 16g   Sugar 9g   Protein 4g   Fibre 0.5g   Fat 9g   Sat Fat 3g   Salt 0.2g

150g (5oz) plain flour, plus extra for dusting
⅛ teaspoon bicarbonate of soda
pinch of salt
25g (1oz) caster sugar
1 medium egg yolk
40ml (1½fl oz) marsala wine (or white wine)
30g (1oz) butter, melted
1.5 litres (2½ pints) sunflower, vegetable or groundnut oil
40g (1½oz) dark chocolate, minimum 70% cocoa solids melted

For the filling
200g (7oz) ricotta cheese
150g (5oz) 0% fat Greek yogurt
40g (1½oz) Nutella
15g (½oz) caster sugar

To decorate
chopped toasted hazelnuts (optional)
cocoa powder or icing sugar (optional)

Note: you can keep the unfilled cannoli in an airtight container for a few days and fill before serving.

Sift the flour and bicarbonate of soda into a bowl and mix with the salt and sugar. Add the egg yolk, marsala wine and butter and mix everything together. Tip out and knead for a few minutes until smooth. Flatten the dough into a disc and chill for at least 30 minutes.

To make the filling, mix all the ingredients together until smooth. Transfer to a piping bag fitted with a medium round nozzle and refrigerate until needed.

Lightly dust a large, flat work surface with flour and roll out the pastry as thinly as possible. Dust the surface with a little flour a few times to prevent any sticking as you roll. Cut out 12 10cm (4in) circles of pastry. Wrap each one tightly around a cannoli mould, wetting each one to seal the pastry together firmly. If the seal is at all loose, the cannoli will come away from the mould as it fries.

Pour the oil into a large, wide saucepan and heat over a medium heat to 180°C/350°F. Drop in a spare piece of pastry to test the heat – it should sizzle immediately and quickly rise to the surface while turning golden. If it browns too quickly, reduce the heat. Turn the heat to medium-low to maintain the right temperature. Line a tray with kitchen paper and have a slotted spoon ready.

Deep-fry the cannoli 2–3 at a time for 1–2 minutes. Remove when risen to the surface and golden brown in colour. Transfer to the lined tray and repeat, then leave to cool completely. Dip the ends into the melted chocolate. Allow to set, and then pipe the filling into the cannoli. Decorate with hazelnuts, cocoa or icing sugar, if desired.

lemon and lavender macarons

Any floral flavour needs to be subtle rather than obvious, such as the hint of lavender here. These are surprisingly easy to make, with few ingredients. Choose a concentrated, good-quality food colouring, so you only need a tiny bit. Too much will change the composition and the recipe won't work.

Makes 15

calories 34   GF   V

Carbs 5g   Sugar 5g   Protein 0.8g   Fibre 0g   Fat 1g   Sat Fat 0g   Salt 0g

65g (2⅓oz) ground almonds
90g (3¼oz) icing sugar
2 medium egg whites (approx.
   60g/2oz)
pinch of salt
40g (1½oz) caster sugar
1–2 drops lavender extract
grated zest of ½ lemon
lilac or pink food colouring
25g (1oz) lemon curd

Note: if you want to save a few for a later time, store in an airtight container and fill just before serving.

Preheat the oven to 160°C/325°F/gas mark 3. Line a large baking tray with greaseproof paper. Using a 2.5cm (1in) round cutter, draw 30 evenly-spaced circles on the paper. Flip it over, so that the drawn side is facing down, but you can see the circles through the paper.

Blitz the ground almonds and icing sugar in a food-processor to a fine powder. Sift into a medium bowl, discarding any bits of almond that don't fall through.

Whisk the egg whites and salt until soft peaks form in an electric stand mixer. Add the caster sugar, a little at a time, and continue whisking until thick and glossy. Stir in the lavender extract and lemon zest. Add a tiny bit of colouring and slowly add more if needed.

Gently fold in half the almond mixture using a rubber spatula, then fold in the rest. Work very gently until evenly mixed. Don't beat it all together to save time.

Transfer to a piping bag fitted with a small round nozzle. Pipe directly into the middle of each circle, allowing the mixture to gradually fill each circle. Lift the piping bag once the circle is full, and repeat.

Dip your finger in water, shake off any excess, and press gently to create a flat surface. Sharply tap the baking tray on your the surface and leave at room temperature for 20 minutes, then bake for 10 minutes. Allow to cool on the baking tray. Sandwich together with lemon curd and serve immediately.

coconut and lime macaroons

These little macaroons are delightful. To make them even more special,
serve them with a little bowl of melted dark chocolate for dipping.

Makes 16

 DF GF V

Carbs 7g Sugar 7g Protein 1g Fibre 2g Fat 6g Sat Fat 5g Salt trace

150g (5oz) dried coconut flakes
100g (3½oz) golden caster
  sugar
4 medium egg whites
grated zest of 2 limes

Preheat the oven to 170°C/350°F/gas mark 4. Place all
the ingredients in a heatproof bowl, mix together well
and place over a saucepan of barely simmering water,
ensuring the base of the bowl is not touching the water.
Stir the mixture over the heat until the egg whites turn
from clear to white. After about 5 minutes of stirring,
they will thicken and coat the coconut flakes. Remove
from the heat and allow to cool, stirring from time
to time.

Line a large baking tray (or two smaller ones) with
greaseproof paper. Using a 7.5cm (3in) round biscuit
cutter as a guide, draw 16 circles onto the greaseproof
paper and then flip it over so you can still see the
circles through the paper. Divide the mixture between
each circle. Press down with the back of a small spoon
to fill each circle, ensuring there are no holes or gaps
in each macaroon. Bake for 12–15 minutes. Beyond
the 12-minute mark, keep a close eye on them, as the
coconut flakes have a tendency to catch and burn.

Halfway through cooking, turn the tray around in the
oven. You will notice the macaroons at the back of the
oven cook a little faster. When they are nicely golden
brown all over, they are ready. Remove from the oven
and allow to cool on the baking tray. Use a palette
knife to help lift them from the greaseproof paper.

These are best eaten within a couple of days.
Store in an airtight container, with each layer
of macaroons separated with greaseproof paper.

sesame, ginger and vanilla biscuits

The flavour of ginger is palate-cleansing and, as such, makes a wonderful flavour to end a meal with. These little biscuits cook so quickly and can easily burn. Keep a close eye beyond 7 minutes in the oven.

Makes 25

calories 55

V

Carbs 6g   Sugar 3g   Protein 1g   Fibre 0.3g   Fat 3g   Sat Fat 1.5g   Salt 0g

100g (3½oz) plain flour
1½ teaspoons ground ginger
50g (1¾oz) icing sugar
70g (2½oz) unsalted chilled butter, cut into cubes
¼ teaspoon peeled and grated fresh ginger
pinch of sea salt flakes
30g (1oz) crystallized ginger
1 medium egg yolk
1 teaspoon vanilla bean paste
20g (¾oz) black sesame seeds

Sift the flour, ground ginger and icing sugar into a bowl and then rub in the butter until the mixture resembles fine breadcrumbs. Add the fresh ginger, salt and crystallized ginger and mix well. Whisk the egg yolk with the vanilla bean paste and then add to the flour mixture. Bring together with your hands and knead lightly until you have a smooth dough (alternatively, use a food-processor to make the dough).

Roll into a log about 23 x 5cm (9 x 2in). Wrap tightly in clingfilm. If the dough is sticky, use the clingfilm to help you roll it. Refrigerate for at least 1 hour (this step can be done in advance).

When ready to cook, preheat the oven to 180°C/350°F/gas mark 4. Line a large baking tray with greaseproof paper. Scatter the sesame seeds onto another small baking tray or a plate. Remove the clingfilm and roll the dough in the sesame seeds. Slice into small circles, about 5mm (¼in) thick. Place on the lined baking tray and bake for 7–10 minutes until the biscuits are golden brown. Allow to cool on the tray before moving. They will be soft when they come out of the oven, but will harden and become crisp as they cool.

honeycomb

No doubt the arch nemesis of almost every dentist, this is about as sweet as a treat gets. For times when a decadent dessert is a little too much, and when all our palate craves is a taste of something sweet, I think a bowl of honeycomb chunks placed in the middle of the table is ideal. Here you will see how to make it decadent and sophisticated, with flavours specifically introduced to counterbalance the intense sweetness.

coffee and cocoa nib honeycomb

This is a post-dinner coffee hit and sweet treat all wrapped up in one.

Makes 35 bite-sized pieces

 calories 36   DF GF V VE

Carbs 8g   Sugar 8g   Protein 0g   Fibre 0g   Fat 0g   Sat Fat 0g   Salt trace

100g (3½oz) golden syrup
200g (7oz) caster sugar
2 teaspoons bicarbonate
  of soda
40g (1½oz) coffee beans
20g (¾oz) cocoa nibs

Make the honeycomb as per the recipe opposite.

When you tip the honeycomb onto the tray, while still hot, scatter the coffee beans and cocoa nibs all over. Allow to cool completely, and then break into bite-sized pieces.

Store in an airtight container. It will keep for up to a few weeks.

sweet and spicy chilli popcorn honeycomb

Use dried chilli flakes if you don't want to blitz your own chillies – this step simply creates a more intense flavour. The combination of sweet and spicy here is quite addictive, especially if you are a chilli lover.

Makes 35 bite-sized pieces

Carbs 9g   Sugar 8g   Protein 0g   Fibre 0g   Fat 0g   Sat Fat 0g   Salt 0.2g

20g (¾oz) popping corn
½ teaspoon sunflower oil
¼ teaspoon cayenne pepper
3 dried chillies, blitzed into
    flakes

For the honeycomb
100g (3½oz) golden syrup
200g (7oz) caster sugar
2 teaspoons bicarbonate
    of soda

Line a large baking tray with greaseproof paper and set aside. Place the popping corn and oil in a medium saucepan and cover with a tight-fitting lid. Place over a medium heat, shake from time to time and leave until all the corn has popped. Tip out into a big bowl, sprinkle the cayenne pepper all over and toss to coat.

To make the honeycomb, pour the golden syrup into a medium, heavy-based non-stick saucepan, and scatter the sugar on top. Place over a low heat and as the syrup heats and becomes more liquid, gently stir to mix in. Leave over the heat to allow the sugar to dissolve; this may take a little while. Try to resist the urge to turn the heat up to make it happen faster; if you do this, the mixture will caramelize before the sugar has dissolved and the recipe won't work properly.

When the sugar has dissolved, increase the heat slightly so that the mixture is bubbling. It will begin to change colour, turning different shades of amber. When it is a deep, almost orange, amber colour and the bubbles are big and popping slowly, remove from the heat.

Tip in the bicarbonate of soda and stir vigorously. The mixture will bubble and quickly expand in size. Tip out onto the prepared baking tray, gently lifting the tray to encourage the mixture to spread out. Scatter the popcorn and chilli flakes all over and allow to cool completely.

When ready to serve, use the end of a rolling pin, or similar, to break into bite-sized pieces. The honeycomb will keep for up to a few weeks in an airtight container.

pistachio, cranberry and chocolate biscuit bites

Chocolate biscuit cake was the ultimate treat when I was a child, and so has a special place in my heart. Here I have adapted it slightly to make these little chocolate biscuit cake 'bites'. If you want to whip up something sweet in a matter of minutes, this is just the recipe. Feel free to play around with the decoration — freeze-dried raspberries and cherries are a great accompaniment to dark chocolate, as are all nuts and dried fruit.

Makes 25

calories 75   V

Carbs 6g   Sugar 4g   Protein 1g   Fibre 0.5g   Fat 5g   Sat Fat 2.5g   Salt 0.1g

100g (3½oz) dark chocolate, minimum 70% cocoa solids
15g (½oz) caster sugar
80g (3oz) unsalted butter, cubed
1 medium egg
100g (3½oz) low-fat digestive biscuits, crushed
20g (¾oz) dried cranberries
30g (1oz) pistachio nibs, roughly chopped (or shelled pistachio nuts, chopped)

Line an 18cm (7in) square, 4cm (1½in) deep loose-based tin with greaseproof paper and set aside.

Place the chocolate, sugar and butter in a heatproof bowl set over a pan of simmering water, ensuring the bowl doesn't touch the water. Stir from time to time while everything melts. Remove from the heat and allow to cool a little before whisking in the egg. It will thicken slightly. Stir through the biscuits and then pour into the prepared tin. Spread into the corners and flatten on top.

Scatter the dried cranberries and pistachio nibs all over and refrigerate until set. Slice into 25 squares and serve with a strong coffee (or espresso martini).

pistachio, almond and rosemary praline shards

These little praline shards are a very simple and elegant way to serve up a little hit of sugar after a big meal. When making the caramel, watch closely as it begins to change colour and swirl the pan to ensure it caramelizes evenly. Be brave – don't take it off the heat until it is a deep amber colour.

Makes about 20 shards

 calories 74

Carbs 12.5g   Sugar 12.5g   Protein 1g   Fibre 0g   Fat 12.5g   Sat Fat 0.2g   Salt trace

vegetable oil, for greasing
250g (9oz) caster sugar
40g (1½oz) almonds, roughly chopped
40g (1½oz) pistachio nuts, roughly chopped
4 sprigs of rosemary, leaves picked

Line a baking tray with greaseproof paper. Brush with a little vegetable oil and set aside.

Place the sugar in a medium, heavy-based saucepan with 200ml (7fl oz) water. Heat gently for 7–10 minutes until the sugar has dissolved, then increase the heat and boil for a further 10 minutes, until the caramel becomes a nice deep amber colour.

Pour onto the prepared baking tray. Tip the tray slightly to encourage the caramel to spread out, then scatter the nuts and rosemary leaves all over and leave to cool. To serve, break into small shards.

salted miso chocolate truffles

If you actually manage to get to the truffle-making
stage of this recipe you are doing well. This ganache
is dangerously addictive!

Makes 30

calories
64

V

Carbs 4.5g   Sugar 4g   Protein 0.8g   Fibre 0g   Fat 5g   Sat Fat 3g   Salt 0.3g

20g (¾oz) soft light brown
  sugar
10g (½oz) golden syrup
55g (2oz) sweet white miso
  paste
generous pinch of salt
10g (½oz) butter
150ml (5fl oz) double cream
150g (5oz) dark chocolate,
  minimum 70% cocoa solids,
  roughly chopped
30g (1oz) cocoa powder

Heat the sugar and golden syrup with 1 tablespoon
of water in a saucepan over a medium heat until
the sugar has dissolved. Whisk in the miso until you
have a smooth paste. Add the salt, and then taste for
balance. Add more if you feel it needs it. Set aside.

In a small saucepan, melt the butter with the cream
and bring to just below boiling point. Small bubbles
will appear around the edge of the saucepan and the
cream will look like it is beginning to quiver beneath
the surface. Remove from the heat and pour all over
the chocolate in a heatproof bowl. Leave for 3–4
minutes and then stir well until you have a smooth,
glossy ganache. Stir in the sweetened miso paste.

Refrigerate until set. Then using a teaspoon, scoop
out small balls of the ganache, each weighing about
15g (½oz), and roll between your palms to make
smooth little balls. Dip each one into cocoa as you
go. Store in an airtight container lined with
greaseproof paper.

sour cherry and raspberry dark chocolate truffles

Freeze-dried raspberries can now often be found in the baking section of larger supermarket isles. However, they are also readily available online. If finding them proves too tricky, these truffles are delicious rolled in blitzed pistachio nuts too.

Makes 26

 calories 78 GF V

Carbs 9g   Sugar 8.5g   Protein 0.5g   Fibre 0.5g   Fat 4g   Sat Fat 2.5g   Salt trace

200g (7oz) dark chocolate, minimum 70% cocoa solids
60g (2oz) unsalted butter, cubed
100ml (3½fl oz) cherry jam
1½ tablespoons kirsch (you can also use brandy)
26 dried sour cherries (approx. 30g/1oz), finely chopped
40g (1½oz) freeze-dried raspberries (or 3 tablespoons cocoa powder)

Place the chocolate and butter in a heatproof bowl set over a saucepan of simmering water, ensuring the bowl does not touch the water. Stir a few times as the chocolate melts and then set aside. Rinse and dry the saucepan and place the jam and kirsch in it. Heat just enough to make it liquid and then blitz with a handheld blender to make it completely smooth. Stir this into the melted chocolate mixture along with the chopped sour cherries and refrigerate until firm. Blitz the freeze-dried raspberries into a fine powder and pour out onto a small baking tray or plate.

When ready, allow the chocolate mixture to come to room temperature for about 15 minutes. Using a teaspoon, scoop out a small ball of chocolate ganache. Roll between the palms of your hands until smooth, then toss in the freeze-dried raspberry powder to thoroughly coat. Mould the truffle into a ball and toss one more time in the powder. Repeat. When all the truffles are done, store in an airtight container lined with greaseproof paper.

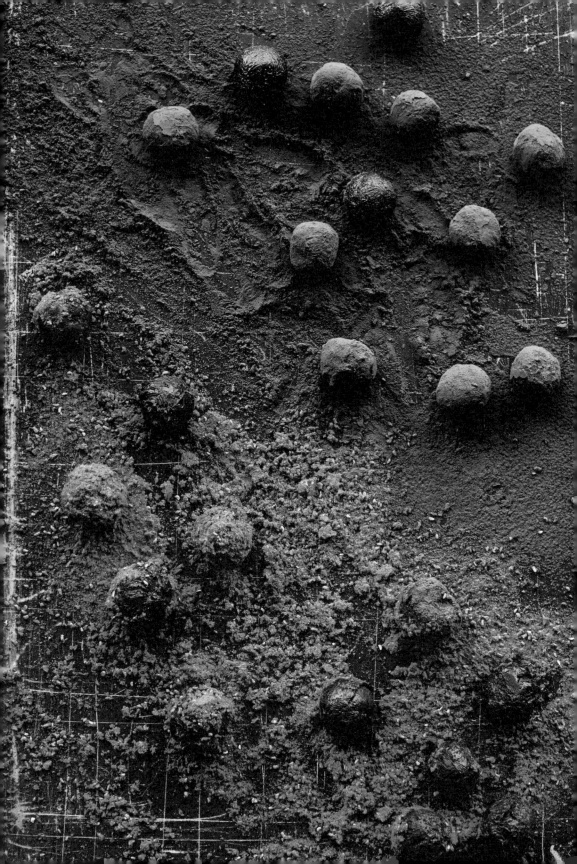

lemon and juniper portuguese custard tarts

Portuguese custard tarts are one of my favourite treats. This is a bit of a cheat's version, using ready-made pastry and lemon and juniper berry custard. Served with a strong coffee, this is indulgence at its best.

Makes 12

calories 162

Carbs 22g   Sugar 15g   Protein 3g   Fibre 0.5g   Fat 7g   Sat Fat 3g   Salt 0.2g

165g (5½oz) caster sugar
peeled rind of 1 lemon
15 juniper berries
170ml (6fl oz) semi-skimmed
  milk
1 vanilla pod, halved and seeds
  scraped out
25g (1oz) plain flour mixed
  with 30ml (1fl oz) semi-
  skimmed milk to form a paste
4 large egg yolks, beaten
butter, for greasing
375g (13oz) packet ready-rolled
  puff pastry
1 teaspoon ground cinnamon
grated zest of 1 lemon
icing sugar, to dust (optional)

Place the caster sugar, lemon rind and juniper berries in a medium saucepan with 90ml (3¼fl oz) water. Bring to a rolling boil over a medium heat, stirring to help the sugar dissolve. Simmer for 5 minutes, then remove from the heat and strain.

Heat the milk with the vanilla pod and seeds in a saucepan until just about to boil, then strain and gradually whisk into the flour paste. Slowly pour in the sugar syrup, whisking continuously. Allow to cool slightly, then whisk into the beaten egg yolks in a bowl. Cover with clingfilm and set aside to cool completely.

Lightly grease a 12-hole muffin tin. Unroll the pastry, dust with the cinnamon and rub it in, then sprinkle over the lemon zest. Tightly roll it up lengthways, like a Swiss roll. Cut 12 round discs, 15mm (⅝in) thick.

Preheat the oven and a baking tray to 240°C/475°F/gas mark 9. Lightly dust a surface and rolling pin with flour. Flatten each disc with your hand (with the swirls facing upwards), then roll out big enough to be pressed into each muffin hole with a little above the rim.

Fill each tart with the cooled custard until ¾ full. Place on top of the hot baking tray and bake for 18–20 minutes. Keep an eye on them – you want the top to be blistered and the pastry to be golden and crisp. Cool slightly, dust with icing sugar, if using, and serve.

raspberry ripple doughnuts

I have never been able to resist a sugar-coated, freshly-fried doughnut. Making your own is as satisfying as eating them. There is nothing especially different about these doughnuts to make them low calorie, except for the filling (yogurt rather than the traditional custard) and their slightly smaller size.

Makes 18 doughnuts

 calories 217 V

Carbs 19g   Sugar 8.5g   Protein 3g   Fibre 0.7g   Fat 14g   Sat Fat 3g   Salt trace

250g (9oz) strong white bread flour, plus extra for dusting
25g (1oz) caster sugar
1 teaspoon (5g/⅛ oz) fast-action dried yeast (from a 7g/¼oz sachet of dried yeast)
2 medium eggs
pinch of salt
55g (2oz) unsalted butter, at room temperature (needs to be very soft)
2 litres (3½ pints) vegetable or sunflower oil, for deep frying
100g (3½oz) caster sugar
150g (5oz) fresh raspberries
300g (10½oz) vanilla yogurt

Place the flour, sugar, yeast, eggs and salt with 75ml (2½fl oz) water in the bowl of an electric stand mixer fitted with the dough hook. Beat on a medium speed until the dough starts to come away from the sides, 7–8 minutes. Add half of the butter and when well incorporated, add the rest. Beat on a high speed for 5–6 minutes, until smooth, glossy and elastic. Cover the bowl with clingfilm and leave in a warm place to rise, until doubled in size – about 1 hour.

Turn the dough out onto a lightly floured surface and knead a little to remove excess air. Divide the mixture into 18 25g (1oz) balls. They will seem small, but will expand with a second prove and when fried. Roll into small, tight balls and place on a lightly floured baking tray, leaving plenty of space between each one. Prove in a warm place for 2–3 hours, until doubled in size.

Heat the oil in a deep fat fryer or large, deep frying pan. If you can, monitor the heat of the oil so that it is around 180°C/350°F. Deep-fry each doughnut for about 1½ minutes on each side. Remove with a slotted spoon onto kitchen paper and then immediately roll in the caster sugar. Repeat with all the doughnuts.

Mash the raspberries into the vanilla yogurt and transfer to a piping bag fitted with a medium round nozzle. When the doughnuts are cool, use a knife to cut a deep incision in each. Pipe in the yogurt mix and then serve as soon as possible.

index

Glossary for US

greaseproof paper – **parchment paper**

baking tray – **baking sheet**

bicarbonate of soda – **baking soda**

caster sugar – **superfine sugar**

clingfilm – **plastic wrap**

cornflour – **cornstarch**

dark muscovado sugar – **dark brown sugar**

double cream – **heavy cream**

golden syrup – **light corn syrup**

icing sugar – **powdered sugar**

plain flour – **all-purpose flour**

semi-skimmed milk – **skim mik**

single cream – **light cream**

vanilla pod – **vanilla bean**